CW00858819

My Stroke

'... just get on with it ...'

A Very Personal Experience

7th July 2014

CHRIS DALE

First published in Great Britain May 2016

2nd Edition July 2016

Copyright © July 2016 Chris Dale

All rights reserved.

ISBN: 1533572623
ISBN-13:978153357?6??

Preview

This book follows the terrifying experience of having a stroke and the remarkable journey made towards recovery; living with the aftermath; and the battle to keep a positive frame of mind, as seen from the victim, his partner and some views from his friends.
It is based on an actual true experience of the writer, but all the names and characters have been changed to protect identities.

Dedication to Gilly

Without your un-faltering support; your belief in
me and your undying love;
I would not have had the courage, nor willpower to
make the recovery I have.

Quotes

These are quotes that really spurred me on to conquer the debilitating state that the stroke left me in:

"You must do the things you think you cannot do"
Eleanor Roosevelt

"Believe you can and you're halfway there"
Theodore Roosevelt

"Start by doing what's necessary; then do what's possible; and suddenly you are doing the impossible"
Francis of Assisi

"Our greatest weakness lies in giving up"
The most certain way to succeed is always to try just one more time.
Thomas A. Edison

Characters:

Peter Hall – *principle character*
Sarah Hall – *fiancé/wife*
Michael (Mike) & Paula Bennet – *Peter's Best friend*
Jane & Andrew – *Sarah's sister & BIL*
Poppy – *Sarah's Niece*
Betty – *Sarah's Mum*
Anne & Charles – *Peter's Sister & BIL*
Vita & Roy – *very close friends*
Libby & Paul – *very close friends*
Suzi & Steve – *Sarah's best friend and hubby*
Serina & Scott- *good friends and ex work colleague*
Zariah & Felix – *very good friends and neighbors*
Robin & Lucy – *very good Flying friends*
Abigail Rich – *Centre Manager*
Susan - *Neighbor*
Luke – *Lives First Responder*
Dave – *Chief Flying Instructor at the flying school*
Jane, Kate & Felicity – *Peters daughters*

Mr. Sudesh Sidra – *Stroke Consultant*
Mandy Slater -*Senior Ward Sister and Ward Manager*
Lisa - *Ward sister & Deputy Ward Manager*
SRN Staff Nurses: Maria, Princess
Morning SEN Staff: Pauley, Jill
Night staff: Carly, Alison
Catering: Pearl & Judy
The OT Team: Janet, Paula, Emily, Wendy, Emma
Speech & Language: Emily and Kate
Diabetes team: Nicky & Jane
Mr. Khan – Stroke Consultant
Dr. Maliki – Diabetic

ACKNOWLEDGMENTS

This book was started whilst still in hospital following the stroke, with Verdana font set on 28 on the iPad as double vision was severely hampering my ability to see.
Sincere thanks go to the staff at the hospital, and to my proof reader, Janet Cook . To my friends and family who encouraged me t write this, and last but not least my wife Gilly for her unending support.

Preface

We take our health and life for granted. But a good life and good health is given to us mere mortals as an honor and the way we treat our bodies is something that few of us think about on a busy day to day basis. It's not just our weight or size; or the food we eat, or drinks we consume; or how we abuse our body, but it's our brain that we also never give credence to as we hustle and bustle through our daily routines.

Never underestimate the sheer power of the human brain. It's a fantastically complex organ that controls every part of your body and we all take it for granted until something like a stroke happens. There are billions of parts to the brain. Different parts of the brain control different functions, and being a total layman I am not at all qualified to make any other comments apart from my own experience which I write below.

My stroke affected the medulla on the left side of my brain–which sits at the back of head at the top of the spinal cord. It's function controls eyes, ears, nose, mouth and balance.

Well pretty important I'd say.

Technically I suffered from a 'medulla Infarct on the left side' of the brain.

What causes a stroke varies widely and is individual from one person to another.

The Stroke Ward at Skidforth General Hospital is a specialty ward for stroke patients for the whole of North Larkenshire and there are approximately 14 of us on the ward, both male and female, and each very individual, in terms of what type and severity of stroke and other complications we each have.
I understand from the Stroke Consultant that mine was caused by a combination of high cholesterol, diabetes, being over-weight and a series of personal issues building to acute stress levels that triggered the stroke.

I am also told that I am very young to have a stroke, but there is a trend building for younger stroke victims due to our changing and very fast lifestyles.

This experience has given me a total appreciation of anyone who has the misfortune to suffer from this disability. In addition, it has brought home to me the difficulties a disabled person has in mobility around the community as the day after I left hospital we found it very difficult to do a simple thing like parking the car with enough room to get the walker out of the car and to get me out and in again! People have no appreciation of the frustration this could cause a disabled person when viewed from this side of the fence!

It has also given me an insight into life on a stroke ward and the sheer professionalism and special personal care we get from a team of very special highly trained nurses, auxiliary team and doctors and the amazing job the OT Team (Occupational Therapy) do at Skidforth Stroke Unit.

My name is Peter Hall and I am 60 years old.

Sarah and I have known each other for the last ten years, in fact I fell in love with her the minute I saw her. We have been in a close loving relationship sharing our home for the last five years, living in a tiny village in the Larkenshire Wolds. We had planned to marry in mid-July, but my stroke intervened. We did finally tie the knot a year later! I had been running my own business which I set up eleven years ago, as a Management Consultant in the food industry, specializing in sales & marketing. I also own a flying school – well I set it up eleven years ago as a hobby really; it was originally designed as my retirement project and as I held a private pilot's licence and have been bonkers about flying and aviation all my life, it was one of my dreams. Since my stroke, the Pilot's licence has been suspended, and not sure if I will ever get it back.

My working background is from FMCG (Fast Moving Consumer Goods) working for major branded suppliers. Up to eleven years ago, I was a corporate man working at senior levels in the companies I had the honor to work for.

From a personal background, I was born overseas, coming to the UK to be educated in public school, and apart from yearly visits home until I was sixteen,

I elected to stay in the UK building my career here – initially in the airline business – what a coincidence! I have three grown up daughters from my previous marriage.

Sarah was born and bred locally and has a tight

close knit family, but sadly her father passed away
at a young age, quite a few years ago. With her
mum Betty, she has an older sister and brother and
a younger brother – all married with family. They
are a fantastic warm, loving family who have
welcomed me into the fold with open arms.
Sadly, both my parents are no longer with us, and I
miss them terribly.
My father, died of pneumonia ten years ago. He
walked off the golf course and was rushed into
hospital with chest pains and died ten days later. It
was very quick and sudden. He was a very talented
man and good at business having had a
distinguished career in engineering, including a
spell working with the government, retiring at
sixty-three.
As he was always travelling abroad, and worked
long hours I hardly ever saw him as I grew up, and
missed those important years incarcerated in a
boarding school.
I only got to know him after he retired, and found
out more who he actually was, and not this man I
held on a pedestal for most of my life. He was
eighty-four when he died – so he had a very good
life.
Following my father's death, we moved mum
down to Cornwall to live near my sister.
Sadly, my mother passed away following a massive
stroke when she reached 84 years of age, six years
ago.
She simply missed my dad. I have a lovely older
sister Anne and a niece and nephew, all with
families of their own.
I am very sad that mum never met Sarah. In fact,

she didn't know about her as we kept our early relationship quiet from most people. The scary experience I had was on the last time I saw mum, about a month before her stroke. As I was leaving to go back home, she took both my hands in hers and looked me straight in my eyes and said to me in a very determined way:

'Peter, follow your heart, I know you are going to be very happy' with a knowing look in her eyes

She knew that my marriage had been very unhappy for a long time and was on the rocks, before I had met Sarah, but she didn't know that Sarah existed, nor did my sister!

'What do you mean mum?'

'You know perfectly well what I am talking about' her grip on my hands was tight as she looked straight at me.

How spooky …. How did she know?

Mothers intuition I suppose, but she somehow knew I was having a relationship with Sarah.

I asked my sister if mum had said anything to her, and she said no.

Mum would have loved Sarah, as she didn't get on very well with my previous wife or family, which was sad as it made life very difficult for me.

So I have a few regrets where my family are concerned, but the up side is that Anne adores Sarah – she is the sister-in-law she has never had.

Months before the stroke I am; (amend that); was a work-a-holic, and would think nothing about driving forty to fifty thousand miles a year and work a typically 17-hour day.

To put this into perspective, a typical week would include driving to Glasgow on a Monday, with three to six meetings planned; then down to London on a Tuesday, driving round the North Circular road meeting customers and maybe Exeter on Thursday, calling into customers in Bristol or Bath on the way down -thus clocking up three to five thousand mile a month.

This was mostly motorway driving leaving at stupid o'clock in the morning and getting home well after eight or nine at night, with local driving once I got to my destination.

These trips were always under some pressure with loads of phone calls, as with modern technology Bluetooth mobile phones through Parrott or the built-in car system meant you were talking all the way up and back. Then once home there was usually at least two hours of e-mails and administration, meeting reports and action notes. Then there would be times when I would be able to fly my plane to an appointment if the location was a long drive away with no prospect of having multiple meetings. This probably happened twice or three times a month, especially if I got a call to make an impromptu meeting at a customer's request, with no time to plan other calls. An example of this is the 45-minute meeting in Swansea with a customer, where driving would mean a six hour drive each way – but the flight time was only one hour and forty minutes. Swansea Airport was a ten-minute taxi drive away from my customer – so it was an easy decision to fly!

The Channel Island, Isle of Man and Northern Ireland were all destinations I would also fly to as it was more economical to use my Piper Warrior than fly commercially. But then I loved this, and partly the reason I started the flying school eleven years ago!!!

Looking back now, whilst writing this, its sounds a totally ludicrous way of life, but that's what I did, and of course, eating on the hoof from fast food and motorway meals added to the weight issue. No wonder my body gave in!!!

To be fair, and I have to add here, that I also love food, wine and beer – and – yes – I am over weight! So there is a classic recipe for an un healthy life style, I hear you say!

In the build up to our wedding day, we encountered several 'events' that tested our resolve as a couple

and proved that we were in a very solid, loving relationship. Any other couple would have buckled at the pressure we were under or re-thought the whole relationship, but not for us!!

Maybe the negative stress that I was under over the previous two years from both my business commitments; my final divorce negotiations together with a very difficult relationship with my three daughters who have chosen to dis-associate themselves with me; the failure of the sale of my marital house and a large bad debt incurred by a toe rag who failed to pay his bill at the flying school; all contributed toward the eventual stroke. On the positive side I was looking forward to finalizing our forthcoming wedding plans.

Who knows!

Eight weeks before our planned wedding day, Sarah was rushed into Grimswell hospital with kidney stones and needed an operation to remove on that had got stuck, which meant her being in hospital for a week, and a week of convalescing at home.

During the two months before the stroke, I had been experiencing small bouts of dizziness and double vision, which normally passed after 3 to 5 minutes.

Occasionally if driving I would pull over and rest until the dizziness went before continuing.

I went to my GP and following blood tests showed that my blood sugars were high and cholesterol was up as well – potentially diabetic.

So I elected to control this through diet, and at 18 stone 8lbs I was and have been overweight even at 6 foot 3". But it became evident that these dizzy spells were in fact TIA's (Transient Ischemic Attacks) and the advanced warnings of the forthcoming stroke. (see the facts on a stroke detailed at the end of this story)

I have to say that I never suffered these dizzy spells whilst flying, maybe because the concentration was different, plus you can't use your mobile phone to make calls, so one's focus is on flying!! Does this mean that focus and concentration whilst driving is taken for granted or arrogantly accepted!

I went on the "Caveman" diet in the middle of June thinking this would also get me in shape for our forthcoming wedding. The Caveman diet is basically the Atkins Diets without any sugars at all. In other words, if you can kill it or catch it – eat it and anything grown above ground, but no grains or pulses or pasta; no fruit, sweets or nuts.

Yes, I believe that I have become diabetic, albeit boarder line, but I have to accept this now, so

perhaps I did not want to believe that I was!! And yes, we have hereditary high cholesterol levels in my family – which I never took medical care of.
So the diet I went on was tailored to control blood sugars and the cholesterol levels, whilst reducing my weight and supposedly keeping me healthy. I cut out alcohol as well, but this was the hard part of the diet. It worked as I did lose weight!
By the time of my stroke, my sugars had reduced to normal levels and my weight down to 17 stone. I felt very well and my new weight more acceptable.
As I leave hospital my weight is down to 15 stone 12 lbs. and now determined to keep this and control my diet!
The day before the stroke, on Sunday, I flew my Piper PA28 aircraft up to Carlisle with my best friend Mike, to take a very good customer's daughter for a flight around the lake district as a very special birthday present. Mike is a Commercial Pilot and instructs for my flying school as well, so he took her, her mum (my customer) and her sister for an hour's flight around the lakes as a lesson. It made her day and Judith my customer was very grateful, but very shocked when she found out that I had a stroke the next day.
Whilst they were flying I took a walk around a Vulcan Bomber and several WW2 jets that are on a static display museum at the airport. The Vulcan was open to the public so I was able to climb into the cockpit. It passed the time.
It was a beautiful day and the flight back to our local airport at five thousand feet was very smooth

and the visibility was incredible, so it was a very uneventful but enjoyable flight back that took an hour, arriving at around 5pm.

I was very relaxed on both flights and thought nothing of it.

Never in a million years did I ever think that within fourteen hours of landing my plane, I would be in a critical condition in hospital.

This is the unknown quantity of one's health, what is just round the corner, you never know. I thought I was fit and healthy, with a constitution that could withstand huge pressure and stress as it has been part of my make up for the whole of my life – resilient to everything ….. sounds like an advert!! And of course with the happy, exciting event in ten days' time.

CHAPTER ONE

The First Week – July

Peter - Monday -5am at home

The sun was shining through the curtains and it looked like it was going to be a lovely sunny July day. Only 12 days to go to The Big Day on 18th July, our long planned wedding.

I try to sit up in bed, feeling a piercing pain in my head, thumping over my left eye. An absolute pounder and just what I needed this morning with so much to do this week. I came to bed at 12 after working late planning my work for this coming week. Bloody hell it's only 5am, again. I seem to be waking at 5am every morning for the past couple of weeks.

I turned to look at Sarah still fast asleep next to me looking so peaceful and beautiful.

I settle down, pulling the cover back over me, to try and get back to sleep.

Unusually I do drop off into a very deep sleep – but for only an hour.

6am......I feel as if I am in a rain forest or a

swimming pool.... disorientated .... Dizzy .... I am
so hot and wet through. My whole body is soaking
wet, I mean the perspiration pouring out of every
pore in my body is intense and so are the sheets on
my side of the bed .... what the hell is happening!!
My bladder feels full, so I am desperate to relieve
myself and decide I need to get to the toilet.
This pounding headache is really hurting now over
my left eye .... I need paracetamol, I am so thirsty,
dizzy and I think I am hallucinating. I look up at
the ceiling and its moving, spinning as if I am
intoxicated.

I swing my legs over the side of the bed and sit up
..... the room starts to spin again and I feel so
nauseous. I just sit there for a while trying to steady
myself enough to make the effort to make it
downstairs where the bathroom is in our little
cottage.

What on earth did I drink last night? Sarah went to
bed at 10pm after the film, and I stayed up
planning the week ahead with a "to do" list for the
two main businesses I own; the flying school and
the three main clients on my management
consultancy business with a call list for
appointments.

Did I finish that bottle of red? Did I have something
stronger like scotch? No ... I am positive that I
didn't have any more alcohol but I am sure I only
had a cup of tea.

I attempt to go down stairs ......well .... I stagger
out of bed and hallucinating with vertigo ...I make
it through the bedroom door and almost fall down
the tight spiral stair case in our little 1856 game
keeper's cottage. I bang my head on the low door

post into the sitting room. Turning left into the kitchen area I head for the cupboard to get a glass out and reach for the paracetamol. I am losing focus in my eyes but manage to get two pills out and some water and take them. I am now heading for our downstairs bathroom to relieve myself. The room is spinning and I can't focus, with double vision now, so I sit down to take a wee.

I am very conscious that this is not right…something is so drastically wrong, as I have never felt this way before. Am I having a fit of some kind, or is it flu or something else. I am soaking wet and I am also freezing cold. It's not a heart attack as I have no pain in my chest.

Standing up and getting off the loo is a major problem, I try to stand but my legs won't support me. I crawl on my hands and knees to the stairs and haul myself back up the stairs and fall into bed with a crash.

Sarah by now is awake and asking me what's wrong. I tell her I don't know, and as she switches on the lights and opens the curtains, she is horrified when she sees that I am soaking wet. I try to sit up but I fall back onto the bed and start to have a fit….my whole body shakes uncontrollably and I am getting colder and colder. Sarah starts shouting at me…

"Peter wake up …Peter what's wrong" feeling my brow and touching my chest.

She grabs the phone and calls 999 …. gets through and asks for an ambulance. They keep, her on the line asking her questions about me and telling her not to let me sleep.

All I want to do is fall asleep, again…. I am so tired

and cold and just want the shakes to stop …. the pain over my left eye is getting worse and I can't feel the left side of my face anymore. It feels as if the dentist has injected my whole left side of my face…it's gone completely numb.

Sarah is saying something but I can't focus on her words. I think she is telling me the ambulance is on its way and the controller keeps talking to her on the phone, asking her what I am doing and relaying this to the ambulance crew. They arrive in 20 minutes which is fantastic given the remote Larkenshire village where we live.

Sarah - Monday – 6am at home

I am woken out of a deep dream of my forthcoming marriage to Peter. I was aware that he has gone down stairs, noisily. I look at the time – its 6am –oh no…I have a full day at work today, and its Monday …. Groan ….. was he due in London today? Can't remember. I turn over and ty to get back to sleep.

He comes back to bed…but clumsily, very much unlike him as he is usually considerate and quietly slips back under the duvet if he has to get up in the night. I am going to have to talk to him in the morning – well later this morning!

I can't get back off, and I sense that there is something amiss.

Something is definitely wrong.

I sit up and turn to look at him, then put my hand out to touch him and find that the bed sheets are soaking wet. Peter starts to shake uncontrollably as

if he is having a fit. I jump out of bed, grab the
curtains to let some light in and switch on the
bedroom light as I rush over to him asking him
what's wrong, but he doesn't seem to be listening
to me. I feel his forehead – he is burning up, his
face red and blotchy, and the perspiration is
pouring off him in buckets that is very disturbing.
I am now very worried, but tell myself not to panic.
I pick up the house phone and dial 999.
'Ambulance please' when they connect.
'What is the emergency'
'I think my partner is having a fit or a stroke'
They asked my address and then asked the
symptoms. An ambulance was on its way.
'Please stay on the line Sarah and describe to me
exactly what is happening to Peter so that I can
relay this to the paramedic in the ambulance'
They kept asking me how Peter was and had to
describe his demeanor until the ambulance crew
arrived.
The doorbell rings and I rush down our stairs, its
Luke who lives two doors down as he is the local
On Call Lives Responder.
'Hi Sarah, I got a call to come round. Is Peter ok?'
'Thanks for coming so quickly Luke, the ambulance
is on its way. Please go on up and see him'
I follow Luke up to the bedroom, he takes vital
signs and looks at Peter – tries to talk to him, but no
sensible response. Peter mumbles something
incoherently.
The we see the flashing lights and reversing bleeps
as the ambulance reverses up our drive. I let the
two crew members in and take them up to Luke
and Peter.

Peter - Monday – 6.30am to 10am – From Home to Hospital

My head is spinning and I feel dizzy, disorientated and freezing cold.

I am aware that Luke from the village has arrived but don't know what he is doing here. Luke must be a Lives First Responder as he is asking me questions about how I feel, I try to answer but he doesn't understand me.

I can't seem to focus anymore and my eyes feel as if they are cross eyed as there are two of every one. Two paramedics come into the bedroom – well looks to me like four and the tiny bedroom is getting crowded. They immediately asses my temperature, blood pressure and a general health check looking for tell-tale signs. I realize sometime afterwards, as I am on the road to recovery, that we are fortunate to have Luke, the On Call Lives Responder living in our village, and he helps the paramedics in assessing what is wrong with me. They ask me if I can touch my nose to his fingertip with my left hand; then he asks me to join my fingertips together with my arms extended. These tests continue as they look for the common signs of a stroke.

I don't know which of his four fingers to touch, and as for my own hands – I now have four as well. Hell ….. where's my nose gone …. I can't feel it anymore?? Everything has gone numb.

I am scared shitless!! What's happening to me?

I can hear them perfectly well as they discuss the assessment. They don't know if it's a stroke or a virus, as the tests they have done are inconclusive; there are exercises I can do and some I can't. I try to tell them of the searing pain over my left eye, and the numbness I am feeling down my right side of my torso and the left side of my face, but my speech is slurred, I can't seem to be able to form words that are coherent to anyone, so they don't understand what I am saying.

It's like I am in a large jam jar looking out, I can hear them perfectly well, but they are a blur as my eyes are crossed over and I see double.

And I can't feel anything either …. Apart from the searing pain over my left eye.

They continue to discuss this with the dispatcher to decide which hospital to go to. In the end they elect on Skidforth General Hospital as they have the only stroke crash team and equipment in the area.

I am still scared, where's Sarah? My head is pounding and I am so, so cold.

The paramedics get me into a special mobility chair and they manhandle me down the spiral stairs to the ambulance. Wow these guys are tough and strong!! I am transferred from the chair to the ambulance trolley and they strap me in, close up the doors and we start the very noisy, hard ride to Skidforth.

Don't they build these vehicles with springs at all! I can see the route we take through Castre and Brydges and although we don't have the lights flashing; blues and two's I think it's called, and onwards through Brydges and Majors Hill to Skidforth.

Every hole, every bump, even the slightly raised painted road signs are felt through the rock hard nonexistent suspension.

It brings back memories of my last journeys in an ambulance when I crashed a Piper Cherokee aircraft at our local airport 5 years ago.

I was coming into land after a three-hour flight back from visiting Anne my sister in Cornwall, leaving from Perranporth airfield.

Air Traffic cleared an S72 Sikorski rig helicopter to land in front of me. I was about 3 miles behind it cleared by Tower to continue approach, and I was watching the helicopter in front. Tower cleared the helicopter to land, and I was excepting it to land on all three wheels. Instead of landing it went into a low hover and request a hover taxi back to the terminal, and during those few minutes of hovering, I was on my approach to land at seventy miles an hour, and the gap between me and the helicopter diminished very quickly.

Tower cleared them to hover taxi but by this time it was too late as the down wash from the rotor blades flipped me over, dropping my right wing and smashing me into the tarmac runway at around sixty miles per hour. The little plane skidded to a halt near the fire training area, and I was saved by the tail fin stopping on a low brick wall surrounding a five hundred litre propane gas tank the fire department

used to ignite the training area with. I was truly very lucky that the plane didn't catch fire, and I was able release my harnesses and climb out of the wrecked plane, despite it ending upside down.

In my pilot's log book I have more take offs than landings; and one 'arrival'!!!

On that day we went to Skidforth hospital first as it

was the nearest hospital, then another ambulance took me to Grimswell as the CT Scanner had broken at Skidforth. On the way back, the ambulance broke down at the top of Majors Hill; so we had to wait for over forty minutes for another ambulance, before arriving back at Skidforth General Hospital. On that occasion I had a broken breast bone, ribs and a heart tambourine (a bleed in the heart), as well as head trauma and spent a week in hospital. Could this be related, five years on?

Back to the present; we arrived at Skidforth hospital and straight into the general emergency crash unit. The paramedics debriefed the Doctors and crash team. They still didn't know what was wrong as my symptoms were similar for either a stroke or an infection. They wire me up to the machines. Blood Pressure is well up.

My 'bet noir' – I hate giving blood!! Two nurses have three attempts to get my bloods and fail to find a vein prepared to cooperate, my veins have shrunk or gone on strike!! A Doctor then finally gets a vein on his third attempt…my arms are like pin cushions! They become very much aware of my distinct fear of needles and in particular blood giving, and the nurses can't help but stifle a giggle when they see my feet kicking uncontrollably as the Doctor tries to find a vein.

I hate this …. what's happening to me?

The senior nurse keeps looking at me in a strange way as if she had seen me before but could not recollect where. Then suddenly she turns round to me and says "your face is very familiar, are you that pilot that crashed a few years ago ….. I was on the crash team as head nurse then!!" What a hell of a coincidence that five years ago she was the same senior nurse on duty!

The next stage is to get me urgently into the CT Scanner to see what was happening in my brain. This happens very quickly and I am impressed at how efficient and quickly the whole team here respond. I am wheeled out of the crash unit, down several corridors and straight past waiting patients and into the scanner – having priority over everyone else. Two orderly's help me onto the scanner. The scan is a strange sensation, but it happens quickly and in no time at all it seems, I am back to emergency crash room, where the Doctors and a Stroke specialist are already reviewing my bloods and the scan info.

And they finally confirm that they are 90% sure it's a stroke to the back of the head, an area called the medulla. This area of your brain controls sight, balance, and speech. My speech is very slurred as if I was pissed as a rat, and my left side of my mouth has dropped slightly. I find it very hard to formulate words and my voice box has gone up 5 octaves to a pathetic squeak which the team can only just understand.

They must be so used to this. My mouth is very dry and I can hardly swallow. Any feeling to the left side of my face has now gone and it's exactly like being at the dentist when he injects your gum and you mouth goes numb…imagine that feeling all over the left side going down your middle nose mouth and neck. My right side arms and legs are also numb, a similar feeling to that of my face. I have lost control of my right arms and legs.

The Stroke Specialist is doing more tests, he holds his finger up and asks me to do some simple tasks. Can't use them and fail the finger to nose test, missing my nose and the doctors finger by a mile – I see an imaginary third finger.

But it's the combination of double blurred vision with a spinning sensation in your head that is the worst feeling of it all. I have permanent vertigo, nausea and spacial disorientation, that is constant.

Sarah arrives at the hospital with her sister Jane. She is shown into the crash unit to be with me and holds my right hand, which now has needles and tubes sticking out, and I have a respirator mask on as well.

The Doctor comes back with yet another blood kit and apologizes but they need more blood samples. I HATE GIVING BLOOD!! DOES NO ONE CARE!! He is successful first time on my right arm near the joint which is my numb side so I don't feel anything.

Sarah - Monday – 6.30am to 8am at Home

I watch helplessly as they carry Peter down the stairs in a special chair, and then onto the trolley in the ambulance. The doors close and off they go – speeding down the road.

Luke asks me if I am OK and tells me to go to Skidforth General Hospital. He asks if he can call anyone for me, which is very kind.

I call my sister Jane and she agrees to come and

collect me from home to save me driving. I call my boss on his mobile and fill him in on Peter's illness– he tells me to take as much time off as I need and not to worry.

I jump into the shower and get dressed quickly as Jane is due any minute and I don't want to be late getting to the hospital…. just in case…..?!!

Just in case what?? Just in case he has a heart attack and dies …. just in case he has a bad viral infection …. just in case he has had a debilitating stroke …. before I get to see him one last time?? "Oh get a grip Sarah" I say to myself.

I think of our wedding in ten days-time. We had a small scare only two weeks ago when I was rushed into Grimswell Hospital and had a kidney stone that had got stuck and had to have a small operation to have it removed ….. now this.

It seems as if our relationship is being tested with all these obstacles being put in our way before we get married to each other!!

Oh Peter…..what's wrong with you?

"I love you so much, please don't do this to me" I say out loud

Jane arrives, we pack a few things for Peter, pyjamas, underpants, dressing gown, his wash kit. We jump in her car and drive off as quick as Jane can drive. I give her directions to the hospital. She wants to know everything.

My sister is two years older than me and has been my soul mate ever since we shared a bedroom together when we were little.

I am in a daze not knowing what to expect and petrified about what we are going to find out at the hospital.

Peter - Monday
the rest of the day and night in Hospital

Sarah arrives with Jane and I feel a huge sense of relief for some reason, knowing she is here.
I see her talking to the stroke consultant and she is in tears…they both are…Sarah and Jane – not the Consultant!!
The crash team manager confirms to the Doctor and Consultants that there is a bed available in Acute Stroke Ward. He orders that I am thrombolysied (or thrombolysis), which is two liters of blood thinning serum that is trickled into my system through the cannula in my hand. The Doctor explains that by Sarah's quick actions in calling the ambulance and their quick assessment to get me to Skidforth General Hospital; it got me to them within the four-hour window when process can be used and vital in catching the stroke in its early stages. This will be a great advantage in the recovery process and a better chance for a full recovery as well.
An hour later we are up on the acute stroke ward and the new team of nurses and doctors take over.
 I get my bed position in the corner of the ward which is good and they re-wire me up.
They take observations every 30 minutes for the first 24 hours, which consists of blood pressure, temperature, oxygenation and movement of hands and feet.
Sarah and Jane are there next to my bed. She is holding my hand.

I have no idea what time it is. I can't see as I have double vision, which is making everything as confusing as hell.
They give me water through a syringe into my mouth and it dribbles down my neck. I can't swallow!
They tell me that they will feed nutrients into me by fluids for today and tonight.
Sarah said she needs to go to call people and organize things – I don't understand; I don't want her to leave me.
The Stroke Consultant approaches Sarah and leads her away from me. Jane stays by my side holding my hand. I can just make out that she is crying too.
Sarah come back from her consultation with the specialist:
'Peter, I am going to go home now as I need to call lots of people to tell them what's happened to you. The Doctor tells me you need to rest now and there is nothing else they can do but keep an eye on you. You have had a very severe stroke, but it's been caught in time. I promise to come and see you tomorrow. Please behave my love, and leave the pretty nurses alone!' she leaned over and gave me a kiss and a hug. Her cheeks were wet with tears.
I spend the rest of the afternoon and evening in a daze. Gosh …. I am so bloody tired … in fact it's a level of sheer exhaustion I have never felt before. All I want to do is sleep, but they don't let you sleep as every half hour a nurse comes and takes my blood pressure and other vital signs.
I get a visit from Janet who is one of
The Occupational Therapists who comes and tells

me that she and her colleagues will be working with me to regain my balance and help me to walk again. But I need to get through the next 48 hours first.

What's all this about – don't be silly ….. of course I can walk!!!!

Then after Janet leaves the ward, then comes Emily who is the Speech and Language therapist and she assess my ability to swallow, and tells me that it is vital that I learn a new technique to be able to bypass the frozen side of my throat and use the right side to swallow.

She starts to work on showing me the technique with little syringes of water.

That night I don't sleep at all. We are constantly woken up and there is a hive of activity with the other five stroke patients on the acute ward. Well I was to find out that over the next three weeks in hospital I didn't get more than two hours sleep at any one time!

Sarah - Monday
Late morning on the stroke unit

The team on the ward tell me that
there is nothing more they can do, as it's now a wait and see situation.

The stroke specialist consultant comes up to me and introduces himself as Mr. Sudesh Sidra. He leads me away from Peter.

I look over to Jane who goes to Peters side and takes his hand, talking gently to him.

'Your husband has suffered a severe stroke. It's a

very rare type of stroke which is why we were confused as he didn't show the usual signs. He has had a Medulla Infarct to his left side'

He shows me on the scan he is holding where the Medulla is at the back of the neck on the base of the spinal cord, and the blood clot that caused the stroke.

'We have stabilized him and your quick action to call the Paramedics when you did has saved him. So you are to be praised. Now there is nothing more we can do except keep a close eye on him for the next 48 hours'

They suggest that I would be better off going home and relaxing, and come in tomorrow at 11am. I am reluctant to leave Peter. He looks so scared, disorientated, very pale and vulnerable. For a big very confident and gentle man at 6 foot 3 he seems to be so lost and anxious.

Jane drives me home and talks about what we need to do now. She can help where she can. My mind is spinning with what I need to do, so I start to make a mental list.

First on the list is to call his sister Anne in Cornwall; then his best friend Mike as he can help with the flying school contacts because he works as an instructor for Peter; call his business partners in his Management Consultancy business – hopefully they can deal with his customers ….. my god the wedding plans!!

Where do I start?

When we arrive home, I go straight to Peters office and find his two mobile phones; one is his business/personal phone, the other the flying school. Jane makes us sandwiches and a cup of tea.

She then takes the sheets off the bed and puts them
in the washer – we need to air and dry the mattress
on the side where Peter sleeps as it is still damp.
My sister is a god send and stays with me until
6pm.
Peter is fortunately a very organized man – thank
god. He has files for everything and all his business
and flying school contacts are easily found.
There is a very large file with – WEDDING! on the
spine. Inside is one page with all the contacts, as
well as a financial page showing that everyone has
been paid as well.
The first call is the most difficult – to his sister
Anne – and I am in tears. Both Peter and Anne's
parents passed away four years ago, so he only has
his sister and her family. Anne said she will come
straight up tomorrow. It's an eight-hour drive.
Sarah tells her to come to our house where they
will stay.
Peter has three daughters as well from his previous
marriage, but they have not been in contact with
him since his break up, and besides I have no idea
how to contact them. Perhaps it's something I will
leave to Peter to decide on once he is capable of
rational thought. His sister Anne can also help here
as well.
I spend the rest of the afternoon and into the
evening calling everyone on Peters lists to inform
them.
Each call takes time as they want to know details of
how it happened and how he is etc., so I end up
repeating the same thing over and over again – to
the point of exhaustion.
Fortunately, Mike and David – Peters friends in the

flying school agree to look after the club. I call his three principle clients who are all shocked for us as well. And I call a few very close friends who all offer to help with anything they can do.

I will leave the wedding until tomorrow as I am exhausted.

At 11pm I drag myself up to our bedroom.

Thankfully my lovely sister has remade the bed and put a picture of Peter on his pillow. I burst into tears again and sob uncontrollably.

I miss him so much – why does this have to happen now – just as we are about to get married and have a fulfilled loving life at last.

Peter - Tuesday- Acute Stroke Ward

The night staff change at 07.30am and a new team of SRN nurses, auxiliaries and junior Doctors meet with the Senior Ward Sister and the Specialist Consultant to assess and review each patients case. They approach my bed, and close the curtains around the bed for privacy.

Mr. Sidra looks at my overnight charts on the clip board at the end of my bed and talks to the other Doctors and Ward Sister in a low voice.

'Good morning Mr. Hall – how are you feeling this morning' he asks in a jovial but professional manner. He looks at me and assesses my condition for himself, as I mumble a reply which is incoherent. He simply nods.

'You have stabilized I am pleased to say Mr. Hall.
So today you are going to have a second CT Scan,
then we will insert a saline drip to manage your
liquids as you are getting dehydrated'
'Head pain …. Thumping …… it hurts' I say
pointing to my left eye brow. He understands
'Can we give Mr. Hall some pain killers via the
cannula to relieve his headache'
The team of Doctors with him start to write notes.
'I will see you later today after your scan Mr. Hall'
And he moves off to the next stroke patient – very
efficiently.
They monitor my vital statistics and observations
every hour now.
The tea trolley comes in but I cannot swallow.
Breakfast also comes, but I cannot swallow; besides
I have no appetite at all. I still feel disorientated,
dizzy and my eyes will not focus, so everything is a
double blur.
I just lie there on my bed, thinking about
everything that I need to do, the business, flying
school and what I am going to have to ask Sarah to
do. I am hoping that I am going to be suitably
recovered enough to attend my own wedding to
Sarah. This is a priority and I need to ask the
Doctors what my chances are to achieve this in ten
days' time.
Sarah comes at 1pm visiting time along with Jane
her sister; Betty her lovely mum is away on holiday
and they said that they have not told her yet.
You have no idea how much I have missed her and
just seeing her again makes me so happy.
She leans over me and takes my face in her hands
and kisses me very gently on the lips. Her touch is

soft and so affectionate that a tear comes to my eyes.

They both sit either side of the bed and Sarah holds my hand.

Sarah starts telling me every one she has spoken to and that Anne is coming up soon. She praises my organization and said she found everyone's telephone number, and they all send their best wishes, but too many to say.

I am very cognitive and understand everything Sarah is telling me but have difficulty in saying what I want to say, so I end up trying to write it down.

At the end of visiting time Sarah tells me she will be back at 6pm, and she thinks that Mike my best friend and Paula his wife are coming as well.

By late afternoon they are concerned about my 'fluid' retention, as I have 800 g of fluid in my bladder. A house doctor comes to fit a catheter!! What a most degrading, humiliating and painful experience this is. For those of a sensitive disposition, or basically squeamish, skip this next part!!!

They insert a rubber tube up your willy into your bladder then inflate a small balloon to keep it in place.

The rubber tube goes into a wider tube that is connected to a bag that collects the fluid. When I saw the second tube I cried at the size of it - but not realizing there was a smaller tube in me. It is awkwardly strapped to my leg and every time I move it tugs in my willy. But it does the job and after a few hours I don't even notice it.

However, living with a catheter is another experience! They attached a clip to my leg that holds it in place and this was placed with a very short lead, so every time I moved in bed it tugged, every time I went to the loo it tugged and this was not a pleasant experience!!

Following a second scan that afternoon- there is nothing on the CT scan that is different but does not show the damage to my brain, and Mr. Sidra need to see what part has been affected. He tells me that I am down for an MRI scan on Wednesday or Thursday which is a more in depth picture and will show the back of my brain, together with an echo cardiogram scan to look at my heart and lungs.

I have visitors, but as I am still on the Acute Ward, these are limited visits to two people only for twenty minutes.

Mike and Paula come and see me. It's great to see them but I can tell from his face that my best friend is very moved when he sees me with all the catheters and tubes coming out of me. I am very touched as it shows how deep our friendship is.

Sarah comes in after Mike & Paula have left and tells me everything she has done. My sister and brother in law are coming up at the weekend as the ward don't want too many people in just yet, so Sarah persuaded her to delay leaving Cornwall until Thursday, by which time I should be more stable.

By Tuesday night I am out of the immediate danger of the blood clot moving so they step down the hourly Observations to two hourly. Still you are not allowed to sleep as you are awakened every two hours for the Observations!!

I drink very little as I find it very hard to swallow, so I get a visit from the Speech & Language therapist who shows me how to swallow water and then soft biscuits by turning my head to the left side. This is so difficult to do as you get a real gagging sensation from the food you are trying to swallow.

Sarah - Tuesday

I didn't sleep at all last night. Worried about Peter. A very good friend of ours Vita called me last night to offer her help. She is one of those people who can turn their hands to anything and she said she would come round to the house this morning to help with the phone calls and organization.
Vita mobilized the flying school team to take over with Michael taking day to day management of the flying school mobile phone, including all the bookings and customers. Simon taking financial control and Dave our Chief Flying Instructor managing the flights and rotas, so this pressure was released from me. Although I had spoken to Peter's Management Consultancy customers, Vita also contacted them all so that they were aware he was not available for the foreseeable future.
What an enormous task Vita achieved given that Peter normally does everything and has all the information on his blackberry and computer at home.
The Ward Sister from the hospital rings to tell me that Peter did well last night and is making good

progress. They are a little worried about potential visitor numbers and gently suggest that until he is passed the critical stage and out of the Acute Ward, that we keep visitors to a minimum and suggest direct family only.

Apparently if Peter gets through Tuesday night ok, he is out of danger and will be moved to a four bed ward. Then visitors would be welcomed.

'Peter and I are due to get married in ten days' time. Do you think that he will be well enough to get married by then?' I ask the Ward Sister.

'I would suggest you raise this with Mr. Sidra or one of the Doctors when you come and visit, but given the severity of what he has been through, I doubt if he will be able to walk in that time'

That was a bolt out of the blue!! What …. He can't walk!!!???

'What do you mean he can't walk Sister?' I ask in trepidation

'His stroke has affected his balance, sight and speech so he will need to re-train the other part of his brain to do these basic functions. Speak to Mr. Sidra when you come in. I will let him know'

I decide to call Anne, his sister in Cornwall.

'Hi Anne. I have just had the hospital on the line and they have asked that we keep numbers to a minimum, but only family can visit him until he is through the next 24 hours. Would it be better for you and Paul to come up at the end of the week and stay the weekend?'

'Oh Sarah, that is a good idea, it takes the pressure off you having to entertain us, but Charles is insistent that we feed you whilst we are up there so you won't have to cook for us.

We can come on Thursday night and go to see
Peter on Friday. He won't mind will he? How is the
little bugger?'
'He is doing very well, but did you know he can't
walk. He has lost his balance and he needs to re-
learn how to walk, talk and see again. You will
need to brace yourself Anne as he looks very pale
and thin. And that's fine with Thursday, I will
leave a key under the frog for you, it makes life
easier for me too. Thanks for being so kind Anne,
Can't wait to see you.'
'Don't worry little sis, we will come armed with
plenty of vino as well. Send my little brother our
love'
I feel relieved that I don't have to worry about
Anne and Charles until Thursday.
My sister calls me to see if there is anything she can
do and asks if she can come and visit Peter with me
today. I am so grateful and she said she would
drive me at lunch time to the hospital for the 1pm
visitor's session.
At twelve o'clock, my sister arrives to take me to
hospital.
Peter is still on the Acute Ward and after a short
while I leave him to go and see Mr. Sidra.
I tell him about our forthcoming wedding in ten
days' time and he looks at me with a deep frown
on his face. He takes me into his little office off the
ward and sits me down.
'I have to be very honest with you that Peter is not
out of trouble yet. He has a lot to go through and
he will need to learn how to walk and talk and eat
again and all this takes time. We still don't know
the full extent of the damage to his brain and we

have an MRI scan booked for tomorrow.

This will give us a better insight to the Medulla where the stroke occurred.

His stroke is very rare, with only 5% of stroke victims having this type, so our knowledge of this type of stroke is limited as we don't have enough evidence from previous cases to refer to. We have several specialist consultants coming to see him from other hospitals, for both their opinion and so that they can gain new experience from Peter'

'What does this mean for Peter's recovery?'

'It's a long as its broad at the moment. He is doing very well and has a lot of fight in him, but as for your wedding plans, I am afraid to say that I suggest you postpone them for the time being. He will not recover sufficiently in time I am afraid to say'

I am taken aback as I didn't realize the severity of Peter's condition.

'We will know in the next three to four days what he is likely to be left with, but we always hope that he will make a full recovery. We won't know until we have seen the MRI scans.'

I thank him and go back to Peter in a daze, but with tears welling up in my eyes too.

This is not the news I wanted to hear, but I won't tell Peter just yet.

On the drive home I tell Jane all about the conversation with the stroke consultant and we all agree to call everyone and postpone the wedding.

I feel as if someone has punched me in the stomach, nauseous and sick.

There isn't much time at home as it takes 45 minutes to get to the hospital. But I know that Mike

& Paula are going to see him first at six, so today I can relax a little.

I need to tell Peter about the wedding tonight and get his agreement to postpone. Mike is Peter's best man so I will tell them tonight when I see them.

As I arrive in the car park at the hospital, Mike and Paula are just coming out.

'Hi you two' I say as Mike gives me a hug. I can see that he is very moved.

'How is he?'

'A different man from the one I flew with on Sunday. I can't believe he has had a stroke. He was so happy on the way back from Carlisle, and he flew well too'

'Mike, we are going to have to postpone the wedding. The Doctors don't believe he will be well enough and he has got a lot to go through in the next six months. So I am going to call everyone tomorrow and postpone'

'That makes sense. Is there anything I can do? Please Sarah let me know'

We say goodbye and I go to the stroke ward to see my Peter.

He is sitting up in bed and looking much better. We discuss the postponement of the wedding, which he sees the sense of. I stay with him until the bell goes at the end of visiting hours .

On the drive home my mind is whirling and I am at a loss as what to do first.

I arrive back home and get the wedding file out ready for tomorrow, but decide that I need to relax tonight and re-charge my batteries.

That night I fall into a deep but troubled sleep after sinking a few large Vodka & Tonics

Peter - Wednesday

We are woken at 5.30 in the morning and I am told that they need to take some blood samples first thing at 6am. The nurse also empties my 'bag' and re attaches a fresh one to my catheter tube and re-straps it to my leg.

Then a nursing auxiliary comes with water, soap and towel to give me a bed wash cleaning my face, hands and back. It's a sheer pleasure.

Pearl comes in with the tea trolley and shouts over to me in a joyful voice.

'Nothing for you Mr. Hall until after your bloods'

The breakfast trolley comes in next and everyone gets their breakfast tray except for me.

At 6am a nurse comes in with a small metal tray and looks at me with a smile.

'Now what's all this I am told about you being a bit awkward at giving blood' in a melodic Jamaican accent – this is Princess who is a wonderfully jovial character.

'Let's be having none of your nonsense with me now' she says in her 'sing-song' voice.

She is very good at her job and finds a vein first time round, and the vein listens to her as she successfully takes three vials of blood.

'What was all that fuss about – man. You were ok with me'

'Princess it must be your technique and wonderful bedside manner'

She giggles loudly at this. 'I gotta watch you man'

Princess returns a few minutes later with a breakfast tray of porridge and tea.

'I don't do this for everyone you know, so don't be
getting used to it'
I thank her and look at the tray not knowing if I can
eat it. But just then Janet from the SALT team -
Speech & Language Therapy - arrives to teach me
how to swallow liquid and puréed food. This is a
real education as the left side of my throat is frozen,
and I learn how to take a very small spoonful of
food into my mouth and roll it into a ball shape in
my mouth, turn my head to the left and then push
it to the right side and swallow without gagging!!
And it's not easy!! Well it's part of the re-education
of my brain to re-learn how to eat.
Later in the morning I get a visit from the Physio
team, who explain my programme to get me
walking again. This is the biggie!!!
My speech is improving so I feel more confident in
being able to explain how I feel and ask questions
too.
Another side effect of my particular stroke is that
my body temperature gauge is stuck on cold,
so during my three-week tenure in hospital it's
been the hottest days of the summer
so far and I am not sweating nor am I hot during
the day. At night I am freezing cold and need to
sleep with a blanket over me.
The Ward Sister comes to see me.
'Got some good news Mr. Hall. We are moving you
into your own room for a few days to help with
your recovery. We need your bed in the Acute
Ward too. It will be soon'
Before lunch I get moved into a private room on
my own…..luxury …and with my own bathroom
too – but only for 5 days, as these side rooms are

kept for critical or infected cases where isolation is vital.

Sarah comes at 2pm – she breezes in with a huge smile on her face. Just the sight of her lifts my spirits.

'Wow, look who's landed on their feet. This is very privileged' she bends over me and gives me a big kiss. Her perfume is lovely as usual. She looks fresh and alert and has a lovely light summer dress on. She is beautiful and she is to be my wife soon.

'Honey, we need to talk about the wedding my love. I was speaking to Mr. Sidra and he has recommended that we postpone as you will not be well enough in ten, no nine days' time'

'I have been thinking the same' I answer

'Tomorrow they are teaching me to walk again, that should be fun. Can you call everyone and postpone the wedding until later this year'

'I want a summer wedding honey, so let's wait until June or July next year'

Libby and Paul arrive just half an hour before visitor's time finishes. I try to sit up to give Libby a hug as they are lovely people and close friends. I have to giggle as Libby said to me in a jocular voice:

'Well Mr. Hall – that's very nice of you to flash your catheter at me ….. I have seen some sights but that really takes the biscuit'.

I didn't realize that in sitting up my hospital gown opened up and exposed all!!

Sarah decides that it's not worth going all the way home as visiting hour's end at 4pm and start again at 6pm. She decides to do some shopping locally and get a bite to eat before coming back.

The OT team come in just after visiting hours to asses my stability and balance. For the first time I swing my legs over the side of the bed and with an OT on each side I slowly place my feet on the floor and attempt to stand up. What a weird experience! I feel giddy and my head spins a bit, but the weirdest experience is that although I know how to walk, the simple action of placing one foot in front of the other is gone …. I don't know how to do it. That part of my brain is gone apparently, and we have to re-train another section of the brain to learn how to balance and walk. Plus, the wee bag and catheter start to pull on my willy …. Ouch!

They tell me that it's a slow process as they only want to do 20 minute's exercises maximum each time, but the catheter has to come out first.

An hour later a very attractive blond nurse comes in with a cloth over a metal tray.

'I've come to remove your catheter Mr. Hall. Please don't be embarrassed as I have seen and done it all before' She was assertive and confident and just did the job. It wasn't a pleasant experience and I felt the balloon inside me deflate and she tugged the tube out as well. But the relief of not having that awful bag strapped to my leg and the tube tugging my willy was so wonderful, it felt like a little bit of freedom.

Sarah comes back at 6pm, in fact she was waiting outside since 5.30 but wasn't allowed in as the nurse was removing the catheter tubes.

Just after Sarah comes, our very good friends Vita and Roy arrive with cards and flowers (which are taken away as we are not allowed them in hospital!!). Vita is a live wire and brings light and happiness into my special room. We get told off by the Ward Sister as Sarah's two brothers and their wives, Max and Emma and James and Fiona, arrive as well, so its crowded in my room. I am actually impressed that her brothers came all the way here. It cements my membership of the family!! What a fantastic feeling to have people who care.

That evening after lights out, I think back to Mondays stroke attack and remember how much fear I was experiencing, but after you are processed and under the excellent medical care, one's thoughts transgress into other concerns, or perhaps also fears.

For instance, am I going to be able to walk normally, eat normally and how much will I have to alter our lifestyle to cope with living with the remanence of post stroke.

What about my pilot's licence and my driving licence; will I ever be able to drive a car again! And until a couple of nights ago my crotch region was also frozen, well one half of it – again the right side – will I get any feeling back and will I be able to function down there again?

Although I drift off with so much rattling through my brain, that night I actually get two sessions of two hours sleep … hurrah!

Sarah - Wednesday

I wake with a groggy head, although I slept well. The house phone rings, and I grab it thinking it's the hospital, I am on edge. But it's my boss from work calling to see how Peter is, and to tell me to take as much time as I need and not to worry. It's a great relief.

Jane, my sister, and Andrew, were leaving to go on holiday today, so I give her a quick call. She said that they were prepared to cancel their holiday to be with me, but I tell her not to be so silly and go enjoy the planned time away.

Peter's Blackberry has about fifty-eight text messages on it, I scan them to see if there are any names that I am familiar with, but I can't answer them all.

It just brings home how many great friends Peter has, from the wedding list alone and all these messages. I haven't even looked at his e-mails yet. I make a priority list of things to do, starting with the wedding plans.

I decide to spend the morning cancelling the wedding suppliers, before going to see Peter.

I get a call from Vita asking if she could come to the hospital tonight with Roy.

Everyone I contacted agreed to postpone the wedding plans, without any penalties despite only giving 9 days' notice. As someone said "well we have your money so we are happy to wait". They were also very considerate and compassionate due to Peters bad fortune.

I am just about to leave when Anne calls to see how Peter is and that they plan to arrive tomorrow by tea time. I tell Anne to make herself at home and that the key will be under the flagstone! I of course will be back by 8pm. They offer to cook.

It's a very hot day, so I put on a light summer frock, and boost myself up to be light and happy for Peter. I leave the house for the 45-minute drive to the hospital.

When I get to the hospital Peter looks refreshed and has changed his pajamas too, so he must have had a wash. He has another plaster over his arm….bloods again!.

I know how much he hates giving blood. It stems back to his early days when he was a boy being brought up in Peru and had to have several injections every year against cholera, yellow fever and typhoid. He hates needles of any kind …. Certainly entering his skin.

I tell Peter the plans underway to postpone the wedding and what everyone has said to me.

I have already called the vicar, the venue, the cake, flower and room dressing people and the photographer. All have been very understanding and agreed to hold the dates open.

Later after the pm visiting hour is up I take the opportunity to do some food shopping at Tesco nearby between the visiting hours, especially with Anne and Paul coming.

Peter's private room is stiflingly hot but he doesn't seem to notice. He asks for his Blackberry and his iPad, but I am not having him getting stressed with calls and work. So I refuse him, gently. I later find out that there is no Wi-Fi at the hospital so he could use them anyway.

After the Tesco shop I return to the ward at 5.30, but they are doing medicines and late rounds with the doctors so I have to wait.

Vita and Roy arrive and as usual they are very kind and offer to help

'Sarah, are you ok financially. Can I help in any way with bills or cash?. You only have to ask!' Roy is so kind.

Ten minutes later my two brothers and their wives arrive and Peters small room becomes noisy and crowded.

The Ward Sister appears at the door and tut's loudly so we all can hear.

'Please keep the noise down and we normally only allow four at a time, but on this occasion I will let it pass, as you are in a private room. But in future when Mr. Hall moves to a ward we will restrict his visitors. Also please bear in mind that Mr. Hall has had a major head trauma'

That told us!!! Thankfully they don't stay very long, but it is very good of them to come to see Peter. By the end of the visitor's time Peter was visibly tired – exhausted actually, which I am told is part and parcel of his stroke.

The Ward Sister pops her head around the door.

'Sarah – sorry I was a bit curt before but we can get into trouble if too many visitors arrive. Peter certainly has a lot of friends. Listen – you don't have to rush off tonight – so spend a little more time with him'

'Oh thank you Sister, we have so much to talk about – you see we were due to get married in 9 days' time and I have been advised by Mr. Sidra that Peter won't be recovered enough, so we are postponing the wedding'

'Oh Sarah, I didn't realize, I am so sorry. But you won't be letting him off the hook this easily then' she said with a smile

'No fear of that and this stroke is a miserable excuse to get out of marrying me!' I said in jest.

I stay another forty minutes with Peter, talking

about everything and he again asks me for his iPad.
When I arrive home, I make the spare room ready
for Anne and Charles, and then make myself some
supper and sit down with my lists in front of the
television, with Peters laptop on my lap going
through his e-mails.

It's again late by the time I eventually go to bed –
exhausted.

That night I cry myself to sleep thinking about my
poor Peter.

Peter - Thursday

I am told by the Ward Sister that today is going to
be a busy day, with several of the medical and
physio teams getting me back to normal.

The Cognitive Recognition therapist comes to
evaluate the damage to my brain with a series of
visual and written tests. I get 99%!!! So nothing
wrong with my memory or my main brain
functions ......they actually found something in
there!!!!

The eye doctor comes next to look at my eyes to
look at the severity of my double vision and
dizziness.

It is all part and parcel of the type of stroke I have,
but the muscle surrounding my left eye in
particular is damaged and the cornea is constantly
moving irrationally up and down. So they
recommend I see the ophthalmic specialist and this
is booked into the diary.

Sarah arrives late at 2.15pm and about thirty
minutes after she comes, the Ophthalmic specialist

who after several eye tests cannot correct my left eye with prisms, so elect to cover my left lens on my glasses to strengthen my right eye and rest my left.

They believe that eventually my left eye will relax and the opticians will be able to prescribe a new lens for me. I have a date in August to see an Ophthalmic specialist in Grimswell Hospital, but it will be Sarah and her team at the Opticians that will prescribe the final new glasses. To see again properly will be heaven.

I get a visit from Occupational Therapy team, who take me into the bathroom with a high stool and asses how I wash, shave, clean teeth and go to the loo. I have to do these actions on my own so they show me tips on how to do this so that my brain re-learns these actions. Trying to shave with double vision, which can't focus is a scream!! And can you imagine the loss of dignity as they watch you have a pee to make sure you can cope with this too. Mind you with my double vision when I look down I have two willies' not just one so its pot luck finding the right one!! They gently recommend that for the time being I sit to take a wee, that way my balance and my aim is not compromised!

I also get more visits from another OT physio team, who take me to start in the gym to learn some sit up, back and standing exercises and a bit of Work on the parallel bars. It's very hard as I feel that the floor is sloping left to right. So I tend to lean to the left to correct my balance, which is my weak side, whereas if I ignore this feeling and Stand upright but leaning to the right I am actually standing properly!! Does that make sense? This is going to be the hardest part of my recovery.

I can relate this feeling of disorientation through my flying experience.

When you learn to fly on instruments only, you wear a hood and special glasses that restricts your field of vision to looking straight ahead and all side and upper vision is blocked out so you rely purely on the instrument panel.

This simulates flying in cloud or IMC (instrument Meteorological Condition).

In an airplane in IMC your body tells you something totally different to your eyes and instruments and in my case I tend to fly right wing down. There is an instrument gauge called an AI or Attitude Indicator and it shows you if your wings are level with the horizon and your rudder ball is centered to fly straight. When you turn, climb or decent this instrument has calibrations to give you an accurate rate of turn, climb or decent so that you can fly the aircraft accurately through cloud or on an ILS (Instrument Landing System) when making your approach to land. My re-learning to walk is very similar to flying in cloud, except that I lean to the left! I visualize that I have an Attitude Indicator in front to find my core balance and lose the feeling that the floor is sloping to the left.

Sarah again goes to the shops between the pm and evening visitor's hours, and my friend Serina and Scott pop in as well. They live locally and I used to work with her in my last job.

Anne and Charles are arriving tonight – so I will see my sister tomorrow and over the weekend.

Sarah - Thursday

I am awakened by a text message on my mobile.
It's Anne telling me that they are just leaving
Cornwall.
I have a gut feeling that it's going to be a busy day
and an even busier weekend.
I spend the morning cleaning the house and getting
some basic food ready for tonight.
I also spend another couple of hours on the
computer answering the many e-mails that have
arrived for Peter.
It's absolutely amazing how many friends he has in
both his businesses as well as personally and how
much care they have for him. My Peter is so well
respected and loved by everyone.
I realize that it's time to leave to go to and see him.
When I get to the hospital parking the car is a
nightmare and I struggle to find a parking space.
So consequently I am late getting to the stroke
ward.
Peter has had a busy morning and in no time at all
the Ophthalmic specialist whisks him off for an eye
test. I go with him when I explain that I am a
qualified Dispensing Optician, so I am there during
his examination. His double vision is worse than
we thought and simple prisms will not do the job,
so they recommend blanking one eye out on his
glasses. One eyed Pete!!
Anne sends me a text at five so say they have
arrived at our house and to give Peter a huge hug.
It's a beautiful hot day, with clear blue skies, and
there is a lovely park nearby, with a comfortable

bench seat, which I sit in and watch the children playing. It gives me time to reflect on the last few days and wonder how long Peter will be in hospital. It all depends on how quickly he can become self-sufficient and do all the basics on his own, including standing and walking. I try and contain my fears about us and what he is thinking about our future.

I love him so much that this stroke is irrelevant but how do I tell him.

It makes no difference to me at all and if he is left with some form of deformity, well so be it. It doesn't change his character or who he is. He is a very kind, thoughtful and caring man, who is exciting and terrific to be with. Besides my whole family have taken to him and the fourteen year's between our ages makes little difference. And he doesn't look his age at all anyway.

When I go back at 6pm, Peter is buzzing as he has had his first session with the Occupational Therapist and his first introduction to walking.

He is SO IMPATIENT, something confirmed by the OT leader.

'We have to say that Peter does things at 100 miles an hour. Patience is not a familiar concept for him'

I laugh and totally agree with her!

When I arrive home Anne bursts into tears when she sees me and we hug for a long time.

Charles pours me a strong V&T and Anne has a meal ready.

We spend the evening catching up and talking about Peter and the wedding.

We all retire to bed late, but I am so glad Anne has come as she is so positive and reassuring.

Peter - Friday

Agghhhh !!!! More blood required!! How much more do they want …. Are they short in the blood bank? I HATE THIS!!

The nurse fails three time to find a vein prepared to co-operate. So a Junior Doctor has a go and fails twice.

I am feeling faint and fed up. Finally, Ward Sister comes and scores first time and I give my three vials of blood. Well I suppose experience counts. Then breakfast of Ready Break and honey, which I seem to be able to cope with- just ……..

… it takes time to eat as I have to roll the food into a ball in my mouth – then push it down my throat. I am turfed out of bed and told that I should spend as much time on the day chair next to my bed rather than in the bed, a sure sign that I am getting better.

I also make my way using the wheeled walker to the bathroom to wash and shave in readiness for my sisters visit.

The OT team come and get me at ten am and we go into the gym and here I work on my core center and balance using the parallel bars and exercises on the large padded table. It is very hard as I know what to do but my brain doesn't …. does that make sense? I spend thirty minutes in the gym when the physio says that it's enough. I argue with her as I want to do more, as I feel that I am getting the hang of walking. But they are adamant that I must not over stress myself.

I ask if we can have another session this afternoon,

'we'll see' was the response.

I am taken back in a wheelchair to my room, and I climb out into my chair.

Soon the SALT team arrive with lunch, which is supposed to be lamb casserole but puréed.

Have you noticed how a young baby taking its first mouthful of this puréed food always spits it out!! Now I know why!! I don't know if it's because my taste buds have temporarily been damaged, but it doesn't matter if it's rich beef stew, lamb or pork casserole, minced beef, cottage pie or chicken casserole – as a purée it tastes all the same …. yuk! And everything comes with puréed Brussels sprouts, swede or cabbage …. which I hate!! Well I should state now that part of the side effects of the stroke is that you lose your sense of taste. Smell is there ok but everything tastes the same.

But in truth, the care that the Speech & Language team put in to finding out how you are able to eat and work out the right diet for you is incredible. Because I had a great problem in swallowing, they showed me a special technique in swallowing, rolling the food into a ball in my mouth, pushing it to the right and then with my head turned to the left, which is my weak side of my throat, forcing my good muscles on the right to push the food down my gullet. They put me on texture one for the first week. This is nearly liquefied puréed food. Then I progressed to texture two, which is the same menu but puréed to a coarser texture and so we progress until my throat has re learnt how to swallow food. So my goal is to enjoy a rare steak & chips with all the trimmings!!

At two o'clock there is a shadow in the door way, and before I look up I recognize the perfume …. Its Anne my gorgeous sister and Charles, with Sarah. She stands there looking at me, and I see tears welling up in her eyes.

'What have you been up to little bro' she says with a beaming smile, but little tears in her eyes.

'Anne – you're here, it's great to see you'

She comes in and sits on the bed and gives me a hug, holding my hand. She is visibly shocked when she sees me as I have lost so much weight, and the stroke has given me a grey pallor.

'Sarah has told me what happened to you, did you have any signs at all that you were going to have a stroke?'

So I go into detail about the times leading up to Monday morning. The TIA's I had in the months before that the doctors thought were the onset of diabetes and my weight, and the work pressure I was under.

She looks around the room and back at me. Charles is sitting in the far corner of the room not saying much, Sarah on the guest chairs on the opposite side of the bed.

'So how are you coping Peter; what's it like in here'

'The day starts at 6am with morning meds and bloods. The caterers come with fresh water and then the nursing team come for observations. After that we are turfed out of bed for washing, followed by breakfast whilst the auxiliaries or nurses make the beds. Normally we are all done by 8.30'

'Is it a very long day, are you getting bored at all'

'The boredom' I laugh …. 'Well…to be honest some of the days are very busy with a lot going on from

visits with the many different therapists, scans,
physio, doctors and nurses checking you and the
routines for breakfast, lunch and dinner. Plus of
course visiting hours from 2 to 4pm and 6 to 8pm
and not knowing who may turn up to see you is
exciting, especially when I know Sarah is coming.
So at times it's all go and you don't get bored but
then I believe that at weekends there is
no physio and they leave you well alone. With no
mobile, an iPad with no Wi-Fi and no watch, time
tends to stand still and your brain starts to kick into
overdrive thinking about everything'
'You poor thing, are you getting any sleep at all'
she asks
'Yes and no. There are spaces in time when you just
sit there contemplating or drifting off to sleep in
your chair only to be woken 10 minutes after going
into another dream world by something or
someone'
'How do you feel now, in yourself?' She continues
her interrogation as is my sister!
'I feel so desperately tired all the time. I have no
sensation in the left side of my face and neck and
the right side of my whole body is also numb, I
can't feel any pain or temperature, so when they
come to take my blood for sugar level checks they
always use this hand' I wave my right hand
in the air. 'I can't see properly – this bloody double
vision, which is why they have blanked off one eye,
and I am learning to walk again – which is not
easy'
'Oh Peter, just take it easy and don't rush things,
Sarah tells me you want everything done now …
typical you really, always at 100 miles per hour!!'

'So I am told sis'

'Well Charles and I are here for the weekend until Monday – if that's OK Sarah, and don't your worry about a thing'

Anne is three years older than me, and we were both born and brought up in Peru in South America, but were separated when I was ten and she thirteen to come to the UK to go to boarding school. The best education our parents could give us. So for six years we only saw each other on the flight back home for Christmas.

I hated school in the UK as all my friends had gone to other schools here and I was very lonely in a school that had bullying and the prefects were allowed to use a small whipping cane to discipline the younger school boys if they misbehaved. As I was a 'foreigner' in their eyes I was picked on a lot. Most of the other boys were from parents in the foreign office, armed services, or minor royals, so I was at odds with them. I also pretended not to understand English as Spanish had been my mother tongue up to now, which frustrated the teachers. I did not make life easy for myself!!

On the other hand, Anne loved her boarding school on the Isle of White. She got in with the right group of girls – all from very wealthy backgrounds and was spoiled with trips out everywhere and to all the right events and places.

In the last fifteen years we have become much closer as my last marriage broke down and having met Sarah, Anne fully approved, knowing how desperately unhappy I was with my previous wife, and mother of my three daughters. They took the marriage break up badly and have not been in contact with me since. Not sure if the fact that Sarah is fourteen years younger than me, has anything to do with it.

I suggest to Sarah and Anne that they relax at home tonight and come and see me tomorrow, so that it gives them time to catch up.

Sarah knows that several friends want to come and see me and so she agrees.

After they have gone at four, I feel exhausted and just want to sleep, but the OT team come into my room

'Now Peter, just a short twenty-minute session in the room here with your walker. We want to try you with a static walker, see how you get on'

It's much easier that the wheeled walker and I master its use fairly quickly.

As it's the weekend the physio and SALT teams don't work so you are allowed to relax a bit.

That evening I have several visits from more very good friends, Libby and Charlie, as well as Vita and Roy.

That night, I do get some sleep, but we are woken up at three am with an emergency arrival and a hive of activity outside my door.

Sarah - Friday

I wake up late, and hear Anne or Charles down stairs in our little game keepers' cottage. It's only a small three bedroomed house – well two bedrooms and Peter's office – built around 1850's – but full of character, and we both love it and the village we live in.

I go downstairs and Anne is making breakfast, looking in all the cupboards for plates, food etc. We hug tightly, she is a touchy, feely person – well Peters whole family are, it's their upbringing, they love hugs which is fantastic!

We talk more about the wedding plans and postponement and of Peters work life and things that still need to be done. Anne is impressed at how organized I am.

I am going back to work on Tuesday, after Anne and Charles have gone back to Cornwall.

I will go directly to hospital after work each evening. Peter is going to be at least another two weeks, possibly three, in hospital, so I might as well get back to earning some money.

It's a lovely sunny hot day again, so we all go for a walk around the village and up to the church which Anne hasn't seen yet. En-route we bump into several villagers who ask after Peter.

We leave at twelve to drive to the hospital, Charles offers to drive, which is a relief for me as it's a horrible route. They suggest we eat in the local pub tonight.

We arrive at hospital and have the same nightmare parking, but eventually find a space. As we approach the ward, Anne hesitates and I can feel her dread rising. We get to Peters private room and I let Anne go in first. She stands at the door looking at her brother and I can see the tears start to trickle down her face. Perhaps I should have prepared her for Peters appearance – he still looks very ill and grey.

She breezes in and hugs her brother. Peter is animated and talks in his high pitched squeaky

voice that Anne is visibly shocked at. His paralysis
on the left side effects his vocal chords and he has
learnt to project or force his voice through his
throat that comes out as a higher pitch.

I just sit there and let them chat. I look at Peter and
think how brave he has been knowing that he hates
hospitals, and everything he has been through.

I have been looking for him all my life – Mr. Right –
and now I have found him I am not letting him go,
at whatever cost.

Peter suggests that we don't come tonight, to give
others a chance to come and see him.

My mum, Betty, calls me. She has just returned
from holiday with her friends, and my younger
brother James collected her from the airport. We
agreed not to tell Mum about Peter as we didn't
want to worry or spoil her holiday and James was
to tell her on the drive back from the airport.

'Oh Sarah, I am so sorry to hear about Peter, and
annoyed that you didn't tell me when I rang. How
is he?'

'Mum, we all agreed that it would be best not to
worry you, and he has pulled through OK. Anne
and Charles have arrived and we are going to the
hospital tomorrow afternoon, do you want to come
as well?'

So they arranged for Betty to drive to our house
and they would all go together in Charles car.

That night we go to the local pub for a meal and
being a Friday night the whole village are in, so
they all want to know how Peter is, having heard
about the ambulance on Monday and seen Luke as
well.

Gosh it's wonderful that after being in the village

for 3 years, we have made so many good friends
here that are all very caring and concerned

Peter - The Weekend

I had a disturbed sleep again, and drifted in and
out of a light sleep. At 5am I am awake and it looks
like it's going to be another balmy blue sky
summers day.
I am going to get bored in here, so I have an idea
which I will ask Sarah about when she comes in.
Breakfast and tea come and then the morning ritual
of washing, I am getting better with the static
walker although the catheter is still very
cumbersome and annoying. I hope that its removed
soon.
Princess tells me that there is a small garden
outside the ward which would be lovely to sit in.
She asks about the wedding plans. I find out that
she is from West Indies and has been here for some
time, she is a large lady but with a wonderful deep
sing song accent. I sit by the side of the bed
listening to an audio story that Sarah brought in as
she thought I would enjoy it, seeing as I can't read.
This passes the time away until lunch time, where I
get my baby puréed food. Every morning we get a
menu with our choice for lunch and supper, and all
of mine sound delicious but it's all runny slop.
After lunch, I get a huge surprise. John, one of my
oldest friends whom I have known for 43 years, has
come all the way up from London on the train to
see me, it was a fantastic surprise. John's wife, who
passed away ten years ago was Peruvian, and he

has two sons and two daughters, his eldest is my
god daughter and he is also god father to my eldest
daughter as well.

He is a lovely man and we embrace in traditional
Latin style.

Sarah, Anne, Charles and Betty all arrive soon after
as they struggled to find a parking spot again, and
are also very surprised to see John too.

Betty, Sarah's mum looks very well having just
spent a week in Spain staying at her friend's villa.
She is so sweet and kind and just as a mum should
be.

I have had loads of visitors, some very unexpected,
and so many friends that I am overwhelmed, and
virtually every afternoon or evening someone has
been to see me. Just didn't realize how well liked I
am and what a bloody lucky guy I am to have such
a good circle of solid loyal friends.

I have had so many cards and messages including
flowers, baskets of fruit and chocolate boxes from
my very good friends, all most generous, it's been
fantastic.

Just before Sarah leaves, I ask her to bring my iPad
next time and charger.

'Now Peter, what do you want that for?' she
questions me with a frown

'I want to write up my experiences in here as a
story, and it will keep my mind active and stop me
getting bored.

Please bring it in. I promise not to surf the internet
or look at e-mails, well there is no Wi-Fi here so I
couldn't even if I wanted to'

She reluctantly agrees.

So the weekend is spent with a rolling crowd of

visitors -plus of course Sarah, Anne and Charles –
thank goodness I have a private room!
The medical team are mainly in the Acute Ward
with the latest victims of stroke or associated
aliments. So apart from the two hourly
Observations where the nurses take your blood
pressure and temperature, we are left largely alone.
In between visitor's hours the nursing staff at
weekends are not that busy so they take the
opportunity to talk to us. I discover that there are
50 Spanish nurses contracted in to work here, and
get to talk in Spanish to several of them. Beatriz,
Noelia, Andrea and Javier are on this weekend.
They were amazed that I still had my accent and
my Spanish improved in a short space of time, as it
had been a while since I had used it.
On Sunday the on-duty weekend Ward Sister is
very lenient and agrees to the number of people
coming to see me.
'You are like a famous pop star Peter' she jests on
Sunday after the pm visits 'You have more visitors
that anyone else here. A very popular man' she
winks at me.
'Tomorrow I am afraid we are going to have to
move you to a four bed ward as we need this for
emergencies and there is a terminally ill man who
needs some privacy. So make the most of it tonight'
Sunday lunch time Sarah reluctantly brings in my
black iPad and charger.
As soon as the visitors have left I open up a word
page and set the font to 'Verdana' on size 28 – as
it's the only size that I can see properly through
one eye.
And so I start writing this book, albeit with two

fingers and literally 19 lines of words per page!!
All I am doing is putting words onto a page in a
'Word' document, re-living the stroke and the first
week in hospital. I also try and remember what I
did the weeks before the stroke – so that the
account of my stroke is accurate. I believe that I
have a very rare type of stroke and only 5% of
people suffer from this Medulla Infarct, whether
that is 5% in the UK or 5% worldwide, I do not
know.

I am hoping that my fresh memories of how I felt at
the time and what I have been through – can
eventually help others to understand and cope with
this illness and give the medical profession an
insight from a personal perspective.

As it happens, the first fourteen thousand words I
wrote were published by the Hospital Trust, but
more of that later.

Chapter Two

The Next Two Weeks -July

Peter

On Monday after Observations and breakfast, I get moved into a four bed ward on the far side of the room next to the window; its warmer in here despite the window being opened wide and the breeze billowing in through the net curtains. The ward is bright and has the three special full movement electric beds and one empty space for me as I am wheeled into the room on my bed from my private room along with my wardrobe and drawers that contain my dressing gown and change of bed clothes.

Each bed "station" has a curtain that can be pulled around the bed for privacy, especially when the doctors come for examinations or the nurses have to do delicate or intimate activity.

By your bed side there is a combined electrical sockets and a television/phone/radio/earplugs set up on a huge metal boon that can be moved around your bed head. You have to pay for it of course and it's not cheap either.

I get to know my new in-mates. We have all had strokes to a variety of severity.

I am the youngest at 60, one chap is 61 and he has the added pain of having had his left leg amputated, one chap is 74 and has sadly had a full blown stroke and can't move or speak, and our fourth ward partner is 87 and has had his second stroke but is recovering well – it wasn't as severe as strokes can be and he has full mobility.

We all settle into a daily routine and the second week goes quite quickly.

I get two physio sessions a day, and every time I go into the gym I improve slowly, But I am always asking to do more.

They start me with parallel bars, and I stand up out of the wheel chair and grab the ends of the parallel bars which the OT team have adjusted to my height. Being so tall they struggle a bit to hold me upright, as my tendency is to fall to the left side. I walk precariously up the center of the bars, turn and walk back holding on very tightly to the bars so that I don't fall.

This is hard to explain but the actual act of putting one foot in front of the other is very hard, as I simply cannot remember how to do it. It is the most-strangest of sensations.

'Peter, the part of your brain that used to control balance and walking is no longer operational, and we have to teach the remaining part of your brain to take up the job the part that has been damaged by the stroke.

The only way to do this is by repetitive exercises until your new brain remembers what to do, so we will exercise for ten minutes on the bars each day, before moving on to the walkers' Janet the OT team leader tells me.

'But can I come back here this afternoon and do more sessions. Ten minutes each day is not going to be enough' I argue.

They realize that they have a fighter on their hands and later tell Sarah that I do things at 100 miles per hour and that I am so impatient.

'Yes – that is Peter I'm afraid. I should have warned you before. He will push you to do more than he can cope with – so you need to be very firm with him' Sarah warns Janet.

The rest of the week I get my way a bit and they take me to the parallel bars twice a day for fifteen minutes to practice and I feel myself getting stronger.

Is this how a baby feels as they find their feet??

After five days I have progressed to a wheeled walker and can walk from the ward to the gym with an OT team on either side of me, but walk there on my own. I feel I am making a positive improvement.

In fact if I need the toilet or in the mornings I use the wheeled walker to get to the bathroom on my own, or with a nurse beside me as a guide just in case I fall ….. which I have done several times when my balance goes skew whiff!!

At the end of the first week I progress to a static walker that makes me more reliant on my legs than pushing the wheeled walker and shuffling behind it. In the gym, I am re-gaining my central core and my balance is better as I can stand straight without toppling to the left side.

They use a moving balance ball machine to help with my central core.

It is a large ball that you stand on and it moves

around and up and down at a speed set by the team. Gradually as each session progresses they increase the speed and action of the ball and I eventually can ride the ball without holding onto the bars. The OT team are well impressed!

So for physio on learning to walk again – it's a combination of parallel bars, back and leg exercises on a large foam mattress, the rodeo machine and the wheeled walker.

BUT – they keep telling me to slow down and ask what the hurry is!!

I WANT TO GET BETTER AND OUT OF HERE!!!

I have three CT Scans, three MRI scans and an Echo Cardiogram for my heart.

The constant care and attention given by all the staff and doctors is superb and second to none and they are looking to see what else they can do to reach a conclusion to my treatment.

The weather is superb, a typical July summer – it's hot and humid and everyone complains about the temperature, except for me as I don't feel anything. My personal temperature gauge has been damaged by the stroke.

Every afternoon during visitor's hour's someone comes to see me. Mike and Paula both fly, Mike as a commercial pilot and Paula as cabin staff. So when they are not rostered they come in to see me knowing that Sarah is at work. On Fridays its Sarah's day off – so she comes at 2pm to 4pm then goes shopping till 6pm and returns to see me. Everyone wheels me out in a ward wheel chair to sit in the lovely garden just to the side of the ward. It is maintained by volunteers and has a nice shady area as well as bench seats amongst rose beds. It's

also nice to sit out here in the evenings when its cooler too, if my visitors are up to wheeling me out. Sarah always breezes in looking gorgeous and waves hello to my fellow in-mates. By the end of the second week, one of the "in-mates" says every time Sarah arrives
'Here comes the child bride' knowing the age difference between us. Fortunately, and typically Sarah, she sees the funny side of it and does not take offence.
As I get to know the others, we do have some fun though, especially with the nurses
I am the most mobile with the chap next to me also quite mobile, but he and the other two have to wear nappies at night as that cannot get out of bed. Two need the crane to lift them onto commodes for ablutions.
The worst part of a shared ward is sleeping at night…..well lying awake listening to the snoring, farting and other bodily noises is something you can conjure up in your own mind. You are basically not allowed to sleep!! For instance, there is a bin in the ward that all paper towels and debris goes into and it has a very heavy lid that when opened is allowed to crash shut, with a very loud bang which makes us all jump with fright – especially at 3 am in the morning!! It's enough to give someone a heart attack!!! I have vowed to fit them all with little rubber feet so that when they close they don't make such a loud dim. I have suggested this to the Ward Sister!
Then the trolleys are noisy, no one whispers at night but talk normally and with each patient requiring different treatments and observations,

plus the coughing fits, burping, farting and patients getting ill at night, you can't do anything but live with night life on a shared ward.

During the second week, my neighbor gets discharged as he is now well enough to go home – lucky chap. However, a strange young man was moved into our ward and into the bed next to mine, with an unknown illness – not a stroke, as the other wards were full.

He has a vomiting illness where he had not eaten for at least 10 days and keeps retching up bile every 20 minutes. Apparently he had a Chinese meal that must have had some sort of salmonella and he lost 2 stone in 10 days from this. I feel very sorry for him as he is only 40s and he cannot help himself. He is on a drip and they keep sending him for scans to find out what's wrong but cannot bottom it. The problem is that I have a vomit phobia and I get put off my food when he starts and so I have taken some meals in the discharge lounge. At night it's even worse as he retched all night long and I feel like joining him.

After two days and nights, he gets moved out onto another ward, and I meet three new in mates and strike up a good friendship straight away. It's a weird sort of camaraderie as we are all from different walks of life and wide age differentials but we have one common bond, to get better and out of hospital back to our home and loved ones. The 18th July would have been our wedding day and when Sarah comes to see me at 2pm, she tells me that there is a surprise organized later on that afternoon.

With the full permission of the Senior Ward Sister, we had a little get together in the gardens, with close friends to raise a glass of non-alcoholic to toast what would have been our wedding day. Sarah looked beautiful and Vita made her a flower band for her hair, and brought me a carnation and three stemmed roses for Sarah.

Paul & Libby and Zariah & Felix brought the non-alcoholic drink and glasses. Felix also made some Rhubarb Cordial mixed with sparkling water and ice …deliciousness, and Paul brought Elderflower and something…. lovely and refreshing! Vita bought a "non-wedding" cake and plates. We had Mike (my best man) & Paula, Vita & Roy, Felix & Zariah, Robin & Lucy, Jane & Betty, Serina & Scott and of course my gorgeous Sarah and me.

It was a lovely afternoon to celebrate what would have been our BIG Wedding Day with our close friends and family.

They all stay for about two hours and I get to chat to them all and Sarah and I have our pictures taken. Some of the ward nurses and Doctors join us – albeit very briefly to have a glass of sparkling grape juice and some cake, and everyone thinks it's a wonderful idea.

Both Sarah and I have something to look forward to – and we vow to plan our actual new wedding date sometime in the summer next year, we can't wait.

Every opportunity I have to type my experiences into my iPad I take, whether it's in the early mornings, midday, night or at three am.

Everyone is curious and want to know what I am doing with that black computer thing.

The staff are also interested and the Ward Sister asks me directly what I am doing.

'I am writing up notes of my experience of the stroke to maybe write into a book sometime in the future.

It passes the time of day and kills the boredom. Do you want to read it to make sure nothing derogatory is written?' I offer showing her the iPad.

'Good grief Peter, that's very large print – you must be writing hundreds of pages with that size'

Dr. Jones is also interested in what I am writing and reads the first few pages where I describe what I am going through when I have the stroke. He has an idea.

Later that week I get a visit from the hospital secretary who asks if she could read the finished story with a view to publication to other stroke victims. I am chuffed to bits.

The North Larkenshire and District NHS Foundation Trust did eventually publish my first booklet for use with other stroke victims and for the medical profession in this area. And the Stroke Association have taken a copy too in PDF format to use for other stroke victims.

By the third Monday I am progressing well with the physio and they have moved me to a walking stick that has four feet on the end which in effect is designed to slow me down so that I take smaller steps to walk and my balance has improved dramatically.

This is progress and my time on the bronco machine (balance ball) and my stepping exercises help me find my core and my balance. Here I feel real improvement although still a bit wobbly when I get tired.

On Tuesday of week three I am moved onto a Soft Diet Texture E menu, which means my first transition towards eating normal foods. Yippee!! By the weekend I am only on four hourly Observations so now well into recovery stage. I am encouraged to become more independent and only need supervision with going to the loo which needs two to supervise with my walker, and physio is two or three short sessions practicing my core and balance. It's coming together and I feel increasingly confident every day.

Dr. Jones, one of the teaching doctors, asks me in week three if I would be prepared to allow some student doctors in their first and second year to practice on me. I understand from one of the staff doctors that my particular stroke is quite rare and they only get a few patients a year with Medullar Infarct on the left side. So my symptoms and my body are a great opportunity to increase their knowledge first hand. I am very happy to help out as I have friends of both my daughters and my own who have been through medical training and to be able to practice on live case is vital to their training. Plus I learned a hell of a lot from Dr Jones myself about the central nervousness system and how very complicated the brain and spinal column is.

My most unexpected and biggest surprise that week, was my youngest daughter Felicity, comes to see me on the third Saturday. That made my heart soar!!

I had been several years since I had last seen Felicity and we talked about what she was up to

and a little about my stroke and how it happened.
She only had a short time, as she had come for
another appointment for herself, but decided to
come and see me as well. I has so pleased that she
had made the effort and I asked her if she would
promise to keep in touch.

Alas – that was the last time I saw her.

My eldest Jane is in South America and I have
received Facebook messages from her. She should
be back in the UK by the end of July and I am so
hoping she will come and see me with Kate my
middle daughter, who has made no attempts to
contact me since her mother and I separated. But
they are all still very upset with me in the manner
that I left home to be with Sarah, it's still all too
raw.

It hurts me deep down inside my heart that I have
no contact with my three beautiful daughters. I
love them, but they don't understand how
unhappy I was, and how this has changed so much
with Sarah in my life. One day ….. I hope, they will
come back into my life.

The staff at this hospital on this particular ward are
all, without exception, the most superb human
beings I have ever met. From the boss – the Senior
Ward Sister and Ward Sisters, to all the Staff and
Auxiliary nurses, to the ward assistants and the
catering and cleaning staff and of course the
doctors and consultants.

The care, warmth, humor, understanding, help and
love given by all these lovely people is infectious
and just shows how well run this ward is.

And they all work so very hard, diligently,
professionally and effectively. All with good

humor.

The doctors are excellent and actually give you the time to explain what is happening and take time to answer your questions and concerns too. They are professional and so very thorough.

A very special and huge thanks to the OT team. Wow, they are brilliant and they instilled so much confidence in you that it makes the whole re-learning process a lot easier. Don't get me wrong …it's tough and you don't initially believe that you will re-learn how to eat, swallow and walk but their dedication to giving you all the motion experiences gets you there. And to pep up your own determination and will power as well!!

Sarah

Anne and Charles leave by ten on Monday so that they are not too late getting home. It's an eight-hour drive for them, and they will stop for a break at the new Gloucester services run by the farming family.

I am preparing to go back to work tomorrow, as there is little more I can do at home, and not knowing how long Peter will be in hospital means that I need to get back into a routine and become busier to avoid falling into the depression pit.

Peter is moved out of his private room and onto a four bed ward with other stroke victims.

He seems to have settled down and is working hard on his exercises to regain his mobility, and his speech is improving as is his ability to swallow – all good signs.

Peter is doing ever so well and every time I go and see him I try and get an update from one of the specialists, either a doctor or a physio. They all praise his sheer determination to get better, which for them is a real benefit as most of the stroke victims tend to just give up and become cabbages. Peter on the other hand talks to anyone who will listen about his flying and how he is determined to get back into the air. He is a breath of fresh air for the ward as it encourages the other "in-mates" as he calls them.

I get a call from Vita who has an idea about the 18th July, which was the day Peter and I were due to get married. She wants to ask the hospital if we can celebrate the day with a few friends in the garden area. She thinks this will boost Peters morale and wellbeing. I agree and think it's a great idea.

The two weeks pass fairly quickly as we all settle into a new routine.

Sometimes after work Jane and mum come with me to see Peter, but every day I get a text message from friends asking if its ok to pop in and see him, mostly in the pm sessions, which works for me.

He is certainly writing about something on his iPad as its always on his bed when I come in. God only knows what he is up to now, always got something going on, which is why he ended up here in the first place, doing too much like a whirl wind.

Every night when I get home I am shattered, but have problems sleeping in our bed without him there. I really miss him.

I arrive home after the special celebration in the

garden patio of the hospital, our non-wedding celebration as Peter calls it. Vita had done a fantastic job organizing everyone, and a cake as well. Ward Sister insisted on three things; no alcohol, no noise and restricted to fifteen people. I had a hair garland and flowers and Peter sat in his wheelchair with a huge lopsided grin on his face. Ward Sister and some of the nurses came out to see us too which was really nice of them.

By the end of the third week in hospital, Peter is walking unaided with a static frame and a few steps with a walking stick. Its great news because this is paramount before they let him home. He passes all the other self-help tests, such as making himself a cup of tea and toast in the mock kitchens just off the ward, and his toiletry as well is all unaided now.

I am looking forward to his home coming, but also have a small doubt in my mind about how I am going to cope as well.

I receive a text from Felicity, Peter's youngest daughter asking if she can go and see him on a specific date. I said to her he would love that, but if she did she must keep the contact going and not just drop him again. I agree to stay away as well and steer everyone away from that particular time, so that they have time to talk together.

Peter's spirits are sky high when I see him later, and all he can talk about is Felicity and how pleased he was that she came to see him. He also secretly had high hopes this would eventually lead to a resumption of a strong father/daughter relationship.

Little did we know that he never saw her again

despite her promising to go back and see him.
Together with the silence from his other two
daughters, who I know he thinks about all the time
and he misses them as well, this devastated Peter.

Chapter Three

Home Assessment & Discharge
End of July - August

Peter

On Thursday 25th July I was taken by car to my house by Emma and Kate for my home assessment review. They dress me in a tracksuit top and bottoms, but it's another warm day so don't need much more. As Emma and Kate have never been to our village before I have to direct them on the best route there, and it takes about fifty minutes. When we arrive, we were met by Lorraine from Louth Stroke Community Care and Jane & Betty (Sarah's sister & mum) have also come to watch and report back to Sarah.

The object of the home assessment was to review my ability to continue my recuperation at home and free up badly needed hospital beds. They would make sure that our cottage was suitably equipped and that of paramount importance was that I would be safe.

They looked at how I was able to move about the house with my walker, using the kitchen area to reach for cupboards, cooker and fridge; using the toilet; sat and got up from the settees; went up the stairs to bed and use the upstairs loo as well.

We went into my office, but I kind of guess Sarah would put a padlock on this door when she goes to work to keep me out!!

The team were very happy with my ability to move around our tiny cottage and the assessment went very well. They agreed on where to fit grab handles and bars that I needed to get in and out of the shower and on and off the toilet seat; high chair seats in the kitchen to help me when cooking and what equipment I would need for mobility. So apart from the slope of the drive (I am told in no uncertain words that I can't sit on my walker chair and scoot down the drive!!!!!) where I need a bar rail fitted on the steps to the house, I passed the assessment with flying colors. So I am hoping for a release home by next Wednesday. Sounds like I am being released after serving a sentence!!!

It was a fantastic trip out after 18 days in hospital and I think that Emma & Kate enjoyed the outing as well as we live just on the edge of the hospital catchment area, so it was further than they would normally go. Plus it was great to see Jane & Betty, who were very apprehensive.

On the way back, we took our time as they had never been out this far before and loved the surrounding countryside; they ask me about the wedding and how Sarah was.

'Sarah has been the most wonderful person in the whole world. I always knew she loved me, but this just shows how much she does and I feel the same way for her. She is my rock.

She has dealt with the whole episode so brilliantly and taking a heck of a lot of pressure in her stride'

I said to them with so much pride.
'Did you know that she single-handedly organized all my business side, informed everyone and kept everyone in the loop. She also called everyone involved in the wedding to postpone which was a lot of work to do. She is just the most marvelous girl in the world, beauty, brains and a heart full to bursting with love. I love her so so much words don't exist to describe how I feel about her and I can't wait to rearrange our wedding date'
Emma & Kate could feel my passion and love for Sarah and knew I would be in safe hands when I got home. They told me it would take a week to fit all the bars and equipment and I asked if this could be accelerated.
'Typical of you Peter – always want things done at 100 mph. Poor Sarah, you must be a nightmare to live with' Emma said jokingly …. Kate and I laughed.

Sarah

I am at work and get a text message from Peter, the first I have had from him in three weeks. It feels strange.
"Hi Honey, I am at home with the Home Assessment team and it looks good for me to come home next week. They say it we don't need too much equipment in our home. See you later Pxx"
I feel elated, my spirits lifted at the thought that he will be home soon.
I am under no illusions that it's not going to be easy and Peter is going to feel very frustrated, so

need to be as supportive as I can.

I text back "That's great my love….can't wait. See you at 6.30 tonight"

I phone my mum and sister to tell them the news and get back to work.

It takes about an hour to reach the hospital and as I am working a late shift I don't finish work until 5.30pm.

I walk into the stroke unit at 6.30pm and the Ward Sister tells me that they needed to clean the ward room – so they have moved Peter into the next ward.

I breeze in and one of the in-mates shouts 'here she comes …… Peter's child bride….hi Sarah'

'Hi Bill… are you still behaving yourself??' I say pointing at him with a wink.

Peter looks much better with colour in his cheeks. The outing to our home did him a lot of good, and a little bit of the old Peter is back. I am so happy …. For him and for me.

We talk about the weekend and hopefully that he will be discharged by the end of next week.

Peter - Discharged!

My release from hospital came through on Tuesday 29th July, three weeks and two days after my stroke, following confirmation that the equipment had been installed in my home, the OT team were happy that I could cope in the kitchen and bathroom without assistance, and the team on the stroke unit started to prepare me for Discharge. Sarah brought me my clothes in anticipation of my

release on Monday night and took away the PJ's and all my bits and pieces, but as she had to work on the day I was able to go home, my best friend Mike and Paula agreed to pick me up and take me home and wait until Sarah got back from work.
We woke up that Tuesday morning at 6 am, I was told to wash and change into my casual clothes after breakfast and not to get back into bed.
I had to wait most of the morning for the various medical personnel to get all my papers and files ready for the doctors to sign the discharge. I also got a special machine - a blood glucose monitoring system - that takes my blood and tells me what my blood sugar levels are, and all my different medications to take home.
It turned into a long morning and time dragged by, as I found myself clock watching with so much excitement that I was finally going home after 3 weeks in hospital. I really wanted to go home, but you know there was a small bit of anxiety about leaving the safety and care of the hospital and the superb team of nurses, careers and doctors that I had got to know so well.
It was quite an emotional time when I left as many of the nurses, the OT team and auxiliaries came to say goodbye and gave me hugs and kisses, it was very moving. Sarah had brought several boxes of chocolates and a couple of cards for me to write a huge thank you to the care team.
It felt very strange being out of hospital and in normal clothes again.
The ward sister came and told me that I will be ready to leave in an hour, so I called Mike and Paula to let them know. They were on their way to

the hospital anyway and would be there shortly. I
suggested they park around the back where the
ambulances collect patients as there was a fifteen-
minute waiting time to collect me.

On the way home I was telling Mike about a car I
had seen at a garage just outside our nearest town
before the stroke and wondered if it was still there.
So as were going to pass the garage en-route home
as we approached the garage Mike turned into the
garage to have a look. Paula was shocked.

'Sarah will be so angry that on the day of your
discharge, of all the days we could pick, you go
looking at cars!!'

'Don't worry Paula, she will see the funny side of
this. We are just looking' I said

Mike added 'we are only looking – won't be long'

Mike helped me look around the car and it was in
very good condition and he said it seemed a great
deal. It is a Mercedes CLK soft top and before my
stroke I had mentioned to Sarah that I was thinking
of changing the old Merc 270 Estate as it had done
197,000 miles on the clock. It was also quite clear
that my stroke will mean a total re-think about my
life goals and I as I will not be driving

40,000 miles a year anymore I wouldn't need a
motorway cruiser, so this CLK looked good fun
with the soft top option and it turned out to be a
straight swap.

And so to home. What a very weird feeling this is,
arriving home three weeks after my stroke. I was
not very good on my feet yet although I had all the
equipment at home with both a static frame
upstairs and another one downstairs, and a
wheeled walker to help me with my walk training.

The first thing Paula did was put the kettle on as we waited for Sarah to come home, the start for me to settling into a new routine.

My first night home with Sarah, was very strange, I have a bath, something I have been dreaming of and - wow - what luxury and pure pleasure that was!! How hilarious and precarious experience as well in trying to get into and out of the bath when your legs and balance are all over the shop. Sarah was at her nerve ends trying to keep me from falling in....what a scream!

It was wonderful to be back in my own bed and the absolute silence!! Expecting to sleep like a log after having no sleep at all in hospital, I was awake for the majority of the night, as I kept on dropping off, then waking up wondering where I was.

Sarah didn't sleep either as we both felt vulnerable, with the knowledge of what had happened that Monday morning and also knowing there were no nurses and other helpers around! However - all throughout the following week I slept like a log and didn't really appreciate how exhausted I was, not just from the stroke but from pure lack of sleep in hospital.

The next day, the first thing I wanted to do after breakfast was to have a haircut, so we went into our local town to go to the barbers.

Parking was a nightmare .... trying to find somewhere to park that has enough room for me to get out of the car and get my wheeled walker out of the boot, then to get to the barbers was very difficult.

Not having a Blue Badge meant that we could not park in the disabled parking so Sarah had to leave the car on a part of the car park that would have been frowned upon by authorities - just to get me out and so I got my hair cut.

Sarah surprised me when she said after the barbers 'How about we go and see that car now'

We went to the garage. Sarah and I took it for a test drive …. well Sarah drove it and she loved it. It's a 9-year-old Mercedes CLK 200 automatic Soft Top with 90k on the clock, but in pristine condition and only a couple of previous owners, so we did the deal, virtually a straight swap for my E270 Mercedes estate that had just clocked up 197,000 miles!!

They were going to valet and service it before delivery but we would have it in a couple of days' time. With the glorious weather we were having I couldn't wait.

Whilst we were out, Caroline from the Local Community Stroke team had called to see me, so we called her to rearrange for the next day.

Sarah takes a couple more days off to help me rehabilitate back home. My walking is precarious to say the least and I am so reliant on the wheeled walker that has a little seat to get round the house down stairs, as I am not confident enough to rely on my stick alone.

I still get dizzy spells if I overdo things – so the sofa in front of the TV is my station for the time being. I can relate to people who become couch cabbages as it's so easy just to sit here with the remote staring at the box in the corner. Instead I use the time to write this story whilst everything is still fresh in my mind.

'Sarah I need to learn to cope on my own – so don't

help me too much. If I fall I need to pick myself up, and I want to make my own tea & coffee's too'

Sarah – Discharged

The day we are told Peter can be discharged, I am having to work as there is no cover for me at work. I feel gutted as I should really be with Peter, but as the only Dispensing Optician available I have a duty to my customers.

Thankfully Mike and Paula volunteer to pick Peter up and take him home and wait till I finish.

The day drags. I keep looking at my watch wondering what is happening.

A text comes in at 12.30 "Picking Peter up now" from Paula

I feel relieved and just have to wait until five pm before I can leave to go home.

At 1.30 another text comes through "You won't believe what the boys are doing…and please don't be angry….but they are looking at cars at the garage in Castrol. I told them its daft and Peter insisted. Pxx"

Initially I was annoyed but then saw the funny side. He told me about the car before he had the stroke and its obviously still there, typical of Peter and Mike to stop.

I drive home as quickly as I could, cursing all the red lights and selfish drivers…don't they know I have to get home!!

I walk through the door, and there is Peter waiting for me on his feet. I put my arms around him and hug him …. it's so good to have him home.

Mike and Paula make a swift departure as they are both rostered to fly tomorrow and are up early doors.

Peter wants a hot bath and it's the most frightening thing I have done as his balance is shot and I struggled to handle his large frame. He almost slips in the bath trying to get out.

I look at him naked ….. he has lost three stone in weight and looks very thin, even emancipated for someone six foot three tall.

After the bath I cook him something soft to eat – scrambled eggs, and we cuddle up on the sofa watching TV. At nine thirty he looks whacked so we go upstairs to bed. Climbing our tight spiral staircase is a challenge but he makes it.

Instead of a good night sleep, we both wake up constantly during the night, so we are exhausted in the morning.

'What shall we do today my love'

'I want a haircut first, then happy to do whatever you want'

'I have an idea of what you would like to do after we get your hair cut'

Driving round our local town trying to find a parking space where Peter is able to get out with his walker was a nightmare, so I just parked on a no-parking zone to get him out and into the hairdressers. I then re-parked the car.

'Come on Peter – lets go and see that car' I say, and Peters face changed and lit up.

At the garage the owner put the soft top roof down and gave us the keys to test drive it. I drove it to Brydges and back and fell in love with the car. It was such fun to drive and although still a Merc it was different from his big heavy E270 Estate which I never enjoyed driving. This car was smaller and more comfortable, well it seemed so. We got back and Peter did the deal.

We get home and there is a note from the OT team who called in – impressive!

Peter is very impatient in wanting to learn how to cope on his own. It left me worried and helpless. I need to go back to work but leaving him at home troubles me so much.

The next day to OT team came to see us and went through some basic exercises for Peter to do and start the long process to rehabilitate him. So we make sure he knows how to get around our little cottage and the OT team assure me he will be ok. They will come probably every other day and in between he will get visits from the Speech & Language therapist as well as the District Nurse – so he won't be on his own. I also arrange for friends to pop round and check up on him.

Peter – Rehabilitating

After nearly four weeks in hospital, I am now out of danger of having another stroke or even a heart attack and the number of pills I pop each day its no wonder!

I still get dizzy spells and my walking is a real struggle; I can lift myself up onto my feet, but finding my central core to gain my balance is still tricky, and the simple task of putting one foot in front of the other even with the aid of the walker is still a challenge.

My vision is blurred and I see double even through one eye only as there is a blanker inside my glasses to block the use of my right eye. The left side of my face is numb as is the whole of the right side of my body, so I have no feeling of either pain or temperature.

But – I am determined to beat this and get back to as normal a life as I can. Sarah and I discussed re-arranging the wedding for May or June next year. This has now become my goal – to walk down the aisle unaided.

The community Occupational Therapists (OT) team will work with me for the next six weeks and they come about two to three times a week, with the SALT (Speech & Language) therapist coming each fortnight to help me with my speech and swallowing.

The Community OT team are very good and give me a series of exercises to do each day to get me rehabilitated back on the road to recovery.

The exercises cover balance, motion, temperature and senses.

I also get a visit from the District Nurse who takes my vital signs and more blood samples ...... aghhhh!!!

I have a standard routine each morning that starts with a slow rise from bed, breakfast, then into the kitchen to fill a bowl with hot water in the sink with cold water - putting both hands into the cold then switching to the hot water for about two minutes, repeating for about half an hour. The next is standing at the work surface and lifting one leg then the other, standing on each leg. Then with each hand. This followed with my walking practice with the static and wheeled walkers up and down the house.

Sarah made a "Sensor" box filed with rice, where about 12 items were hidden which I have to identify by feel with my hands. In the shower I stroke my left arms and legs, then my right arm and legs with a shower mitt to get my feeling back into my right side.

The final exercise was on my face with a tooth brush and make up brushes where Sarah had to do certain strokes over different muscles on my face, left side then right side. All this is aimed at re-training my brain to recognize what sensory areas shown feel like.

Our local vicar kindly brought round a wheelchair to use when we go out, which was a huge help. However, I did constantly make Sarah very nervous as the wheelchair had self-propelled hand grips on the wheels, and I could whisk off on my own causing all sorts of worries about running into cars, shelves and people for Sarah. I have to say that there are a lot of retail outlets that do provide wheelchair use free of charge if you ask at the reception desk and not having a Blue Badge in the early days of release is a hindrance (see Blue Badge section later in the story), but if you call the supermarket or garden center they will give permission to park in their disabled bays.

The Local team were brilliant and would call me at around 10am to make sure I was in.

They apparently had a huge joke about me as I am one of the few stroke victims that they have to call to ensure I am in - as I am lucky enough to have friends who come to take me out! They must see a whole variety of stroke victims and most, as I understand, are very much house bound and self-motivation is a major problem. So I appear to be new challenge for them, as once again, I am told to have patience and give myself time to repair and recover. Because I did do my exercises and they would see me do them on each visit they were happy to let me continue without a daily visit. They did bring different specialists to help me with my balance and started exercises to strengthen my legs which was executed on the bed.

I also got a balance ball to practice my hip movement. So this was quite intense and it was a major contributor to building my confidence and improve my walking.

I was amazed one day 8 weeks after my stroke, when Ahmed made me walk into the sitting room from the kitchen, then told me to walk back without my stick, and so I did.......and walked for the first time unaided. Well I was very wobbly and it was a major event for me, but it was the start of my ability to walk.

It is so important that stroke victims have the ability to be mobile or know that they can get their mobility back, but it takes a very major change to ones thought process and your own self belief that you can and will get mobile again, because at times, you really don't think you are going to achieve it.

It so important to be able to push yourself to do all the exercises that the OT team give you and to keep trying, just 5 or 10 minutes a couple of times a day on your own and after a week or so you will see the improvement you can make.

I did this - pushed myself to do all the exercises and within 14 weeks I am much more confident on my feet and getting around. It means that I am not house bound and when Sarah is on a day off work we always go out somewhere, even if it's to do shopping, or lunch or a very short walk down Thrunscoe sea front. Also friends and neighbors come to take me out and they are always very nervous about how I will cope, but I do because of the practice I do on the exercises that are designed to get you mobile again.

I still do need to use my stick to walk around outside the house, and I inside the house I either "furniture "walk or use the NHS issue walking stick to help my balance. This NHS stick is a little bit short and makes me stoop when walking normally. The NHS don't have a longer stick for tall people.

Sarah and I were in Lowth antique center and found a brilliant very old walking stick made from a tree branch which is the right height and comfortable handle and we had a rubber foot fitted as well. It's an antique so very relevant for me...now I am an antique!!!! It makes me distinguished ...apparently!!

Sarah - Rehabilitating

For Peter's first week home, I take the week off to be with him, as we have several appointments to see the diabetic nurse, ophthalmic specialist and our local GP at Castre Health Centre.

There was a concern that home life would be very

boring, but with the visits from the community OT teams, friends popping in for tea and the continuing exercises made the day's fly by. Peter does get tired very quickly and started to have a rest at around 3pm each day, but also was amazed that when we went to bed at 10 he slept through to 7 the next morning.

We are learning so much more about his stroke and the many different kinds of stroke people have. Peter is very lucky in that the attack he had is a very rare version that apparently only affects 5% of stroke victims, and the Medulla Infarct to the left side effects balance, Speech and sight, so he maintains full use of his limbs and his full faculties. The main issues are with the numbness to the left side of his face and the whole of the right side of his body; arms, torso and legs have no feeling or temperature gauge.

He also has a problem with swallowing so eating is a chore, and his voice box gets very strained if he spends too long talking. He has to force his voice through his voice box to get any volume. Funnily we went to the Harvest Festival service at Rodewelle Church and singing was a real challenge, coming out as a high pitched squeak!! There have also been several "accidents" - so much so that I wanted Peter to text me at 4pm each day to tell me that he is ok and had not had any accidents. For instance, he was conscious that his left ear was full of wax, so he got a cotton bud to clean it …. but as he has no feeling in the left side of his face he accidentally pushed the cotton bud so far into his ear that he pierced his ear drum, causing an infection that spread over his face. This resulted in yet another trip to the GP and a course of anti-biotics.

Then, he has had several falls in the garden trying to get up the steps so we have banned him from enjoying the garden – so he can only sit on the patio unless he has someone with him to take him to the garden seats.

In the kitchen he has discovered the joys of cooking and he genuinely loves to cook meals. This is all well and good – BUT he has had several accidents with the very sharp knives and as he is on blood thinning pills he needs to be careful not to cut himself, as he bleeds and bleeds and bleeds!!

Whilst on the subject of cooking, he has also had quite a number of burns on his hands, his right hand has no temperature control so he can't feel heat.

Once he was softening onions and garlic in a pan on the cooker and some spilled out onto the hob top, so he swiped it with his right index finger without realizing that the hob was red hot. I arrived home from work to find his right hand bandaged with a serious burn. Of course he is right handed, so this affects virtually anything he does with his hand!!

Hot drinks are also a danger as Peter has burned his throat countless times with trying to drink a cup of tea or coffee. So now I have insisted that he either makes a tepid cuppa, or wait until it gets cold before drinking. The burnt throat then created even more problems with his swallowing and eating food as it swelled from the burns!!

I am becoming an emotional wreck and the drive home from work is made in trepidation not knowing what he will have been up to!!

Peter does get a lot of visitors, he is one of these guys who has many great friends, and they all come and see him around their own busy schedule. His best friend Mike is a commercial pilot and works rostered duties so he can be away for a week and home for a week. Mike and Paula (who is an Air Hostess) come and see him regularly. It was a very emotional time when Mike first came to the hospital to see Peter and he was visibly shaken by the stroke. Mike and Peter are very close and he will be our Best Man when we eventually get married.

The community health team also call every other day, both the OT and SALT teams as well as the community nurse.

This is care he will have for the first six weeks at home, so I am happy leaving him at home as I know that most of the time he has people coming to see him.

What I am concerned about is the longer term future, as we don't yet know if Peter will ever be able to drive again, if his eye sight does not improve,

nor will he be able to go back to the job he used to do. So it may be a life changing situation for him. Peter is a very self-motivated man and has terrific will power too, but I can see that he does at times let his guard down and he shows his vulnerability. He gets very tired and still has dizzy spells that worries me.

He wants to give something back to the community, but for the time being until we know what he is capable of doing physically, we just

Chris Dale

have to live day to day.
He is slowly getting to grips with the
administration for the flying school which keeps
him distracted, plus of course his book writing....
Well this book!

Chapter Three

Living with a Stroke
September to December

Peter

Balance is still an issue as I have tripped on the stairs a couple of times – not that Sarah knows and as I still get dizzy spells which means I fall to the left when I lose my balance. I tried to clean up outside by sweeping the drive, but this was just too difficult and I got tired very quickly. I have fallen trying to climb the three steps into the garden - even though I have my stick with me. This is the frustrating side of my incarceration in our lovely home.

It is still a very little known illness, and every stroke patient is different, and their recovery is different as well. It also very much depends on the type of stroke you have, and I am fortunate (if you can use that word) to have had a very rare stroke which only about 5% of victims get. So I will hopefully make at least a 90% recovery, but what I will be left with is not known.

Recovery is very much down to you as an individual, and your ability to be self-motivated to get better.

The Occupational Therapists and Speech & Language teams can help you understand and give you all the exercises to help your brain re-train to do everything that the part of the brain the stroke has killed, but It is still very much down to your own self-belief, your own self-motivation and your own sheer will power to make yourself recover that will determine whether or not you allow the stroke to take over your body and your life or not.

Please don't get me wrong, I too suffer from time to time with some depression and I get very fed up of not being normal...not being able to do normal things, not being able to drive or eat properly and enjoy my food, and not being able to walk around free of sticks and dizziness. For me, my recovery is taking too long.....so there kicks in my impatience. When I am on my own, I sometimes scream as loud as I can, which isn't very loud as I have my frozen throat ..... but just to vent my frustration!!!!!

I have had several hospital outpatient appointments with Orthoptist specialist at Grimswell Hospital to see if a prism could be fitted to my glasses to correct the double vision. The first appointment soon after my discharge was not successful as my eyes were too far out of balance, so I persevered for five weeks in which time my eyes had repaired sufficiently enough for a prism to be fitted that now enables me to read and watch TV without too much double vision. It still makes my eyes tired if I read or work on the computer more than 20 minutes at a time.

We had a disastrous appointment with an Ophthalmic specialist (he was a locum as the Consultant was on holiday) who clearly did not

have my files and had no idea why I was seeing
him. When I told him that I had a stroke a month
before, he asked if I had now recovered, bearing in
mind that
I came in a wheelchair and it took both Sarah and
his nurse to help me out of my wheelchair and into
his special chair for the eye test!! So I asked him
what he thought and questioned his skills at
observation!!? He did some tests on my eyes and
confirmed that the muscles around the left cornea
were dead and would never recover, virtually
sticking a feather into my eye, which I did not feel,
and then proceeded to confirm that I had double
vision and that I should advise the DVLA
which meant I could not drive. Interestingly he
made no tests to ascertain whether I had double
vision or not!! This was not a good experience and
clearly the guy was not interested. To add to the
frustration that day, we arrived on time for our
appointment, but waited over an hour to see the
doctor.
Unfortunately, I have also had my Pilot Medical
certificate suspended, which means I cannot
officially fly a plane as Pilot-in- Command until I
can pass both a full CAA (Civil Aviation Authority)
medical examination, which requires full eye sight
and balance, and I have to re-take my Private Pilots
air test. So this is a goal for some time in the future!
The Stroke unit at Skidforth wanted to do a cardio
monitor of my heart, so I was taken into hospital by
the lovely Felicity (Sarah's best friend) to have the
heart monitor fitted for a 24-hour period.
Well Fliss is a rather gorgeous blond and bubbly
character and our journey to Skidforth from home

was an adventure to say the least! She is a fantastically kind person but her driving skills were rather erratic and we had an "interesting" journey to and from Skidforth. It was very kind of her to volunteer and she did pre-warn me of her driving as it is a well-known and amusing experience by all her friends. I think that the heart monitor must have had a few "high" readings in the 40-minute journey home!!

I am very conscious that I have had a very serious illness and my recovery from the stroke is going to take time. I am told that I am expecting too much of myself, and need to come to terms with the fact that I need to rest every day and lower my expectations on what I can and cannot do.

To pass the time and keep my brain active, I have discovered the pleasure of cooking and it's something I can do that does not tire me and can do it sat on my high chair in the kitchen and take my time. I am learning how to bake cookies, lemon drizzle cake, carrot cake, as well as meals for Sarah and I. So every evening she comes home to a Vodka & tonic, hot bath and a different meal, although she does not complain she does crave ham egg and chips or baked beans on toast every now and again!! It was very fortunate to have fallen ill during one of the best summers we have had and virtually every day through August and September have been glorious.

It's given me the opportunity to be able to sit out on the patio and watch the pheasants, birds and peacocks in the garden.

I can read but only for about 15 minutes or so before my eyes get very sore and tired. Jane –

Sarah's sister brings round some magazines for light reading - women's own etc. so I am getting up to speed with who's who in the celeb world. It is a problem with the font size so normal books and newspapers are a bit of a problem, as I have to focus on the print and it's tiring.

In addition, working on the computer or even the iPad I am using to write this story is very tiring too, and although I have the font on 24, I struggle with the focus even though I had a prism fitted last week which has helped with my vision. I therefore do a short amount of work on either the computer or iPad for about 20 minutes max.

On the day I had my stroke, three peacocks took up residence in our garden, which was a fabulous sight as they kept me company during the day. Two are male with glorious plumage and one is female – plain brown feathers and smaller than the other two. They would come every morning for bird seed that we would put out on the top lawn by the steps, and sometimes on the patio. At times when there was no food they would come right up to the conservatory windows and peck on the door asking for food. Incredible!!

One morning I left the door from the conservatory to the patio open and the female peacock came in looking for food, I came out of the shower to find her about to enter the kitchen. In her panic to get out she tried to fly through the glass in the conservatory and she shat everywhere. Being plant and grain eaters, it was green slippery liquid bile rather than the normal hard deposits we would get from a canine or cat.

But I eventually managed to catch her by placing a

large towel over her, guiding her out of the door, but the mess she left was horrendous and it spread everywhere, so I had to clean up the floor, glass windows and the two cloth covered sofas before Sarah got home.

I have had to have several appointments at the doctors in Castre and I am fortunate to have some really kind neighbors in the village who have taken me up to the surgery, for diabetic eye screening, prescriptions, appointments with my GP and other appointments.

Over time I am hoping that my vision and my speech will improve and return to normal. The medical team cannot say what I am going to be left with but they believe I will make a 90% recovery. Walking, vision and balance are all actions that the new brain can relearn, but it's the throat which controls swallowing and voice box that is something that is not controlled by the brain but is a bodily function. Although I can talk, it is a strain as I force my vocal cords to work and occasionally it comes out through my nose. But it's an effort and this also gets very tiring.

Eating remains my real issue, as it has not shown any change or improvement in the last 8 weeks. It makes meal times a real chore and although I can taste my food, it takes so long to eat, and chew the food until it's well masticated to be able to swallow it using the left head technique I was taught in hospital.

Sarah
Living with Peter and a Stroke

I am living in a bubble.

I go to work because I have to, not because I want to.

I would much rather stay at home and look after Peter.

I go to work very hesitant, I jump every time the phone rings expecting a call to say something has happened to Peter, and I drive home in trepidation not knowing what he has been up to all day.

With Peter's lack of feeling in his right hand, he is prone to burns and cuts without feeling them. He has learnt to cook and has become quite accomplished chef, except for the cuts and burns he gets on his hands!! He suffers with dizzy spells and his walking is similar to someone who has had one too many!! He staggers around like a proper drunk. My heart misses a beat every time he goes up and down stairs. But there is no stopping him.

You cannot criticize his sheer determination and will power to overcome this illness.

He has so much self-motivation it's incredible to watch and I am so proud of him.

He is under strict instructions not to go up the steps in the garden, BUT he does what he wants. The other day, he got his bike out and pumped up the tires, then took the bike to the main road, and tried to ride it – he fell off twice before our neighbor intervened and told him to stop, joking that

Chris Dale

he could borrow their children's stabilizers! He tells
me that his mind remembers what to do, but the
actual knowledge of balance on a bike has gone. It's
a weird feeling.

I know he is very frustrated.

His brain is very active and he wants to do so much
more, but his double vision makes it difficult to
read and see, and his fatigue kicks in mid-
afternoon forcing him into becoming a couch
potato. This is when he gets his iPad out and
writes.

He is also frustrated in not having transport. He
still can't drive and is reliant on neighbors, family
and friends to get him about.

We went to Lowth one Friday with mum, just for
some fresh air and to wonder round the market.
It's a lovely town with some great shops and a
good pub that is the oldest pub in Larkenshire that
serves great food. There is an antique centre at the
back of the town just up from the main square that
is fascinating. We were rummaging around when
Peter called me over.

'What do you think of this?' he asked holding out
an antique walking stick. The best way to describe
this is that it's a varnished quite slim branch from a
tree that has had the end carved out of the main
trunk into a round nob, with a thumb and finger
impression that sits comfortably in Peters hand .....
and it's the right length too. His existing NHS
aluminum stick is too short for him, so he bends
over too much when walking, causing all sorts of
problems for him, none the least looking where he
is going!!

So we do a deal with the center and purchase it for
£28, and go straight to the local cobblers to have a
rubber foot fitted. Peter is ecstatic with his new
purchase and immediately names it 'sticky'. His
posture is improved, he can see where he is going
and it's much more comfortable for him to use.
And He looks so distinguished too!! Adds
character.

Being concerned at Peter's frustration at being
"incarcerated" -as he calls it – in our lovely cottage
for the last six months, a friend suggested that we
should think of a change of scenery and maybe
going away on a weekend break.

 In early December I took Peter on a short break in
Harrogate for two nights in the St George's Hotel
on a special deal I got through the internet. It was
a lovely sunny weekend and the drive to Harrogate
in the Merc was great as Peter was in a very
positive mood. The room was a deluxe superior
double and the large room size and ample
bathroom was easy for Peter to navigate.

We had a great relaxing time with a change of
scenery for both of us, finishing with Christmas
shopping in York on Friday. This was a most
welcomed break and gave us some good exercise
walking around Harrogate and York and being
able to spend quality time with Peter. He went
swimming for the first time since the stroke.
Amazingly it was no different apart from the fact
that in Breast stroke and front crawl he tended to
swim to the left, just like his walking.

My sister Jane and mum help out with seeing Peter
and taking him out sometimes, but for most of

the time he is at home, but I know he doesn't just sit there, he is always doing something.

Peter & Sarah
Blue Badge & Benefits

I have applied for a Blue Badge and after 10 weeks, I found out that they had lost my application form. So I had to re-apply again, but asked that it be given priority, as I really needed it and had waited 10 weeks! Give them their due, they turned it round in a week and I received it in the post a week later.

This is only a suggestion for the government to think about. As a proposal, anyone who has had either a stroke, heart attack or major limb surgery, should be issued with a temporary "Purple" Badge within a 5-week time limit- as part of their discharge from hospital. This would be of enormous help in the early weeks from leaving hospital as the number of appointments require to visit the hospital, doctor's surgeries and supermarkets, town centers etc. when you need to park in a space large enough to be able to open the door wide enough to get out and then to get the wheelchair/walker/walking stick out and get settled is impossible in normal parking spots.

You end up parking the car at the far end of a car park where there is space and then have the task of walking or being pushed a distance to get to your destination.

To have a simple system with perhaps a "Purple Badge" issued with your discharge paperwork would help so many thousands of people and with the limit of 5 weeks gives enough time to apply for an official Blue Badge, if indeed you need one by that time. In many cases, people with limb injuries would not need one after 5 weeks.

The art of claiming your rightful benefits

I am supposed to be very careful not to get very stressed as this was part of the cause of my stroke in the first place. Stress is one of the key factors that I have to try and avoid, but financial pressure is always present and trying to understand and deal with the benefits system is a stressful pursuit to say the least.

It is so overwhelming to find out what help I can get from the government now that I am not working and having been self-employed, my income has literally dried up. Now I know that the authorities have to be very careful with a proportion of society who will try and scrounge every penny they can get and never work, but for someone who is a "fully paid up member of society" having worked all my life from 17 years of age, and never once claimed a penny from the state, it's very disheartening and stressful trying to find out what we are entitled to.

Having had a stroke, one's vision is not brilliant and the forms that are required are plentiful. There are two benefits I can claim, Employment Benefit and PIPs (personal independent payment).

These are not means tested but are payments that we can receive based on whether you can work or not.

The first is paid fairly quickly but it's not much to begin with -£75 per week, the second takes around

26 weeks to be implemented but for both of these we have to get medical certificates from your GP, (which costs money getting to the surgery and then getting the certificate, and you need to do this twice in the first 13 weeks).

So financially we have to fend for ourselves and dig into our hard earned savings, having paid all the tax we have over the years. It's annoying and disheartening to read in the papers and hear anecdotally that "foreigners" arrive in this country and are given housing, food and money almost straight away, yet we - the fully paid up members of the community, have to wait this time and be assessed to how much we get, and have to fund everything out of one's own assets, is a little beguiling. A very helpful lady from Job Centre suggested I talk to the council to see if there is any help I can get with our rates etc., but no - as Sarah works full time and I have more than £16k in savings, we are not entitled to anything from the council.

So I have now had my medical Assessment by the PIP's officer who came to the house to assess what I am able to do, so that they can decide how much I will receive in Personal Independence benefit. The most baffling conundrum is, that it appears the less intelligent you are, and the less able you are, the more money you receive. There were a number of questions asked such as "if we gave you a map and a route to a destination, would you be able to follow it??"

Now if I answered no I would not as I don't know how to do that .... I would get a larger payment than the truth. But at the moment I cannot drive as

I have double vision, so would not be able to read a map to navigate, so in reality – no I can't read a map;
but I was told by the assessor that as I held a pilot's Licence and I drive it means that I could and in normal circumstances read a map, so this makes no difference!! How crazy is this?
I have no idea what I will receive, but it will take the DSS another 8 weeks to make a decision based on a questionnaire that bears no relevance to my personal situation.
 Would it be a good idea if the government had a new system in place, where upon falling on hard times due to illness such as a stroke or heart attack, they enter you NI number, name and DOB into their system, see that you have never claimed a penny in your whole working time and issue you with a £600 a month cash payment, that would be paid for the first 3 months until you have the chance to be evaluated.
Ironically – to cover ourselves during this 26-week period before we received any benefit payments, I drew down some money off my pension – which I paid tax on; and low and behold I get a letter from the DSS stating that my benefits will be halved as I am now drawing a pension!! It took three phone calls and a letter of confirmation from my pension provider that this was a 'one off' draw down to get my benefits re-instated. They are slow to give it to you but quick to take it back!!

Peter - Medical reviews.

My six-week review was held with Dr Abbas at Skidforth General Hospital. I saw the OT team and they were amazed at how well I had progressed in the time since I left them. I have to have another MRI scan as I have some small tears if the blood vessels in the area of the stroke, and as this was a scan taken in the last week in hospital they don't know if the tear has repaired or not.

Otherwise they are happy with my progress, apart from the dizziness I still have. I am told that it's my positive attitude that has been a major facet of my rapid initial recovery, and that I am about 3 months ahead of where I would normally be expected to be after a stroke attack such as I had.

At my visit to the diabetic nurse she took blood samples for the 10-week review and both cholesterol and blood sugars are down to near normal levels which is brilliant news, (Cholesterol down from 7 to 4.4 and blood sugars down from 61 to 45) and my core ratio has also reduced from 5.6 to 3.7 - below normal levels. My weight has settled around just under 16 stone so I have lost over 3 and half stone since the month before the stroke when I started to diet.

Sarah and I were due to get married on 18th July, 10 days after my stroke, and so had to postpone the happy event. Well we are pleased to be able to re-book our day and have chosen 19th June next year as the big day.

This was the only choice out of 4 dates that the Hotel had available and it was very generous and kind of both of them, and all the other wedding suppliers (photographer, cake, coach, singer and band etc.) to allow us to postpone and rebook for next year. We have taken out wedding insurance this time though!

Talking about insurance, we did have our honeymoon insured, however upon applying for the insurance to recover the cost of the honeymoon, we have been declined by the insurers due to the fact that I had pre-existing medical conditions that led to the stroke. By this they have highlighted diabetes and cholesterol. Now on closer inspection of their precise words in their terms and conditions it does state that we had to advise them if we had any pre-existing conditions that were being treated by prescribed drugs or medication, which I was not.

Due to my pilot's license, if I were to take drugs to control my blood sugars, then this would affect my pilot medical certificate, and invalidate my Licence, so I chose to control blood sugars through diet. The battle has started with our honeymoon insurers.

There have been several forms to complete and two visits to the doctors to get the right information and letters to confirm that I was not under any medication for either symptoms and now we wait to see what they say. We are happy to report that the insurance company have finally agreed to pay up and settled our claim outright.

Two weeks ago I had a 3rd MRI scan to see if the veins have healed and the blood clot that caused the stroke has gone.

This will be discussed at my 5-month review. In addition, I have also been to see an ENT specialist about my throat and speech, who found that the left side of my throat is still damaged and I now need a video fluoroscopy scan to see what damage exist for the specialists to be able to outline a process to repair this.

The Five Month Review -is a set back!

The MRI scan showed that the small blood vessels in the Medulla on the left side of my brain above my spinal column, where my stroke hit have not repaired and there is a tear and a blood clot still embedded in the vein. The thermalized procedure I had when I first arrived at hospital has not worked 100% and although it has protected the main part of my brain, it did not penetrate the small blood vessels in the back of my brain where the stroke happened.

They are not sure what to do and have taken advice from other stroke specialist consultants who have said that because of the rarity of my stroke they have very little experience of what drugs/treatment would work to dissolve or release the blood clot. They can change the clopidogrel blood thinning drugs to something stronger such as Warfarin, but are reluctant to do this as they don't think it will make any difference.

They can only recommend that we continue with the drugs I am taking at the same dosages for another 4 months and review in March.

This blood clot and tear is what is causing the dizziness and balance problems.

It is also linked to the numbness feeling in my left side of the face and right side of my body as the nerves pass through the medulla on the left side. An operation in that part of the brain is too complicated, and they are not sure what the future will bring.

I am at risk of having another stroke if I allow stress levels and blood pressure to increase, so they do not want me to work to any great extent. I explained what I was doing currently and they were happy with that except for flying and driving, which they have advised I leave for another couple of months.

Mr. Sidra was concerned about the dry skin on my hands and ears and wanted to know what drugs my GP believes are causing this, as these may need to be changed.

My throat problem will be left to the ENT experts to resolve and my eye sight should in their opinion improve. The sensations and temperature control in my right side should continue to improve as well but it depends on what happens with the blood clot.

Strokes are still a little known medical problem and in my case the rarity of my condition is giving them problems in deciding the right course of treatment. I have to take life easy for the next 4 months and keep stress levels low. It is vital that I keep my blood
sugar levels between 4.8 to 7 and my cholesterol to below 5. So watch the diet and the weight - don't lose too much weight and control the diabetes and cholesterol.

Mr. Sidra was impressed with my walking and the general improvements I had made and said that I was ahead of where they would expect me to be having had the size and severity of stroke that I experienced. He was encouraged by my positive attitude and my determination to get better, but warned of allowing this to turn into pressure on my self-leading to increased self-imposed stress levels.

As part of my on-going treatment at home I keep active and avoid being sedentary but don't over exercise to cause stress levels. Yes, I can fly commercially and I can go swimming but avoid anything such as cycling or running as this will raise blood pressure.

So this is a huge disappointment as I was hoping that the veins had repaired and the blood clot removed. I now have to spend the next 4 months taking things very easy and being mindful not to become stressed and raise my blood pressure. I am hoping that the doctors will be able to come up with another solution to repair the damaged veins and disintegrate the clot. But it's rather worrying that the experts are unsure of what to do.

With Christmas round the corner, there is a lot to do at home to prepare for this - tree, decorations, preparing some food, cakes and biscuits, and sending out Christmas cards etc.

Sarah – Medical Reviews

Attending medical reviews with Peter is difficult as most take place during the day in the week and require Peter to attend Skidforth General Hospital and it is very difficult to get time off work to accompany him. These meetings are very important and as Peter is still unable to drive, we rely on my mother, sister or friends to take him.

Peter does take copious notes in each meeting and we talk in the evening about the review and I have to keep him buoyant and objective. Peter sometimes comes home despondent and dejected, and we talk up the positives.

This was especially significant after the five-month review which Peter saw as a major setback.

He was disappointed that they did not clear the blood clot and that this will be inside his brain, lodged there for the rest of his life. He was also despondent that he will not see much improvement in his limbs as he still finds walking a problem. He has set himself several targets;

a)   he wants to be able to walk me down the aisle once we are married;

b)   he wants to get his driving Licence back;

c)   he intends to get his Pilot's Licence back – which I am not sure about.

These are all good goals to reach for and they drive him on.

He needs to overcome his double vision and at the moment this is still a long way off, as the test he has had with the ophthalmic specialist show that one eye is still damaged and is just within the limits of a prism to help him see properly, but nowhere near the requirement to drive.

Peter is also getting some 'feeling' back in his groin and he is starting to get more sensual feelings as well. I am a little cautious about getting amorous as I still feel it's too early for him given what he has been through, but very pleased that everything works ok in that department!

Peter - Christmas

Well six months down the line and I am getting to the stage where I am resigned to accepting that my recovery to full normality is going to take much longer than I originally thought, if indeed I do recover one hundred percent.

The doctors want to leave me to continue to rest and recuperate for another three-months, or until the end of March, before they make any further decisions on treatment. They have now totally ruled out surgery to remove the blood clot as this is too dangerous being so close to the spinal cord. The paralysis on my right side may never recover, nor the left side of my face, so they are building me up to come to terms with these facts.

But if I can recover then I will. My eye sight is still wonky and the prism in my left glass of my specs drives me crazy.

It also means that I am not going to be able to drive until at least the spring, and my thoughts go to our forthcoming wedding in June, by which time I know at least, that I will be able to walk Sarah down the aisle after we are married.

We send out the wedding invites for a second time, and hope that people can make it. I did send an e-mail to everyone last month forewarning them of the new planned date for the wedding so they had advanced notice.

Christmas is nearly upon us, and this year I am totally reliant on either Jane, Sarah's sister, or on the internet and home deliveries!!

When I get a delivery, I wrap it up there and then

and then have to find somewhere to hide it so that Sarah does not find it as she rummages around the house. I want everything to be a complete surprise for her, and this year I want to spoil her as she has given up so much to be here for me.

Jane comes to the house every Saturday to help with the cleaning and she is excellent company. We get on very well and after she has finished cleaning we sit in the conservatory or, during the summer months, on the patio having a cup of tea and a cake that I have made for her, and we chin wag about everything.

She is also becoming my confidant as I can talk to her about personal matters -especially the hurt I feel from my estranged daughters. Having a daughter, she understands this, not that Sarah doesn't, don't get me wrong; but for some reason I don't like to discuss my thoughts about my girls to Sarah – she had enough burden with me!

Christmas Eve, Sarah takes me to our local pub, which is normally a two-minute walk and a five - minute stagger back!! But today we take our time as my walking is slow with 'sticky'.

The whole village are in the pub and we have a great time chatting to everyone.

I am given a bar stool to sit on and am treated like the walking wounded – but I like the attention, especially from all the women!! Sarah keeps an eye on me – well on what I am drinking, but sadly my days of downing five or six pints are gone, as two is sufficient for me.

After a couple of hours in the pub, I start to get tired and feel myself getting a little light headed or dizzy and disorientated, and the pub seemed to be getting very hot and noisy, so I nod to Sarah as a signal that I have had enough, and she comes to my rescue, suggesting that we should go home now. Everyone, sees how physically tired I look and we bid them a very Happy Christmas and leave.

We go back home to a wee dram before going to bed and cuddle up under the warmed duvet.

Christmas morning is a bright and sunny day, and Sarah and I get up, have breakfast and then open some personal presents from each other and from my sister. We spend a very pleasant morning, before we go to church for the 11am service.

We spend Christmas lunch and afternoon at Betty's house and the whole family come. It's a wonderful time, as Betty is a great cook and we all muck in. Everyone opens their presents with care and admire the gift, and they are all amazed at how I have been so secretive in the purchases of my gifts.

Sitting around in the pub, or in the church or at home, the reality is that I am an invalid at the moment and I just need to understand this, but deep down inside me I don't believe that I am. It's frustrating. Everyone is so kind and are always at hand to grab me or hold me, when all I want is to cope on my own. Does that sound selfish?

Sarah – Christmas

Peter is up to something – I know it as every time I come home from work he looks guilty.

I know Christmas is looming and normally I am quite organized and start to get Christmas presents ready well before – even start in the summer. Peter sent all the cards out to all our friends in November which kept him busy for a week.

He did very well considering his eye sight and getting used to hand writing without being able to feel the pen in his hand. How he does it I don't know, but he just gets on with it.

He has been out with my sister Jane a couple of times shopping but he never does buy anything when we are out on Fridays, or when I have the odd day off.

I suspect that he is getting a lot delivered to the house from the empty packages I have seen in the bins!! So he's not that clever after all. But he is still up to something.

He has also sent out the wedding invitations, which again was quite a feat for him. In his usual way he has a master list on his computer of all the guests we have invited and the seating plan, hotels we are using for people staying, and the plans before and after the wedding.

We don't intend to go on honeymoon until the Monday morning after our Friday wedding. Peters sister and brother-in-law are staying nearby until Sunday and he wants to maximize their time up here.

He is a great planner and I am sure that our wedding will run like clockwork. The original plans from last year are still applicable now except for the dates, and Peter has everything in control. As Peter cannot fly commercially we have elected to honeymoon in Norfolk and find an idyllic hotel just outside Cromer that has cottages in the grounds

and is half board with gastro food each evening
cooked by the owner who is a professional chef.
It turns out to be even better than we thought and
we extend our stay with them for another two
nights. That's how good it was.

Christmas Eve we go to our local pub, which is
packed and very noisy, but Peter is loving the
attention and the couple of pints of beer he drinks.
It's a special treat for him.

We get home from the pub after a few hours as
Peter get tired very quickly. Instead of going
straight to bed, we sit by the fire sipping a glass of
port and just enjoying the peace.

'I can't wait until June when we get married my
love' Peter whispers in my ear giving me a kiss.
'It's going to be the best wedding ever, and I am
going to walk you back down the aisle without
'Sticky' I promise' He adds, and I know that he will
achieve this.

We go to bed and snuggle up to each other before
falling into a very pleasant and peaceful sleep.
The next day Peter is awake and staring at me
asleep.

'Moring gorgeous, Happy Christmas' and he gives
me a kiss. What a way to wake up!

It's a lovely bright chilly morning and Peter goes
downstairs to light the fire in the sitting room,
whilst I make breakfast.

We then open a few presents from each other and
Anne – Peters sister, rather than taking them all the
way to mums house to bring them back again.

Church bells ring at 10.45 so we get ready to go to
the Christmas service at 11am, its only just round
the corner and its where we will be getting

married, we love the 11 century-cum- Norman church.
After church we drive to mums house and spend Christmas Day with mum, my sister, her daughter and husband and my brothers pop in as well.
It's a lovely day.
Peter's first Christmas after his stroke and although he is mobile, he is still not that confident on his feet and he is very conscious of his eating routine and swallowing in public.
But we have a wonderful Christmas with my family. Anne – Peter's sister – calls us at mums too so that was very good of her to include her new family.

Chapter Four

January to May
Peter

Firstly, it very much depends on how I am feeling, as every morning I am either fresh and feeling positive or I am tired and dizzy with problems focusing, and pain in my left eye.

Sarah goes to work every morning but has Friday's and Sunday's off in general. So I always get up and have breakfast with her, then get washed and dressed. It's a routine discipline I force myself into – so that I get a purpose every day. It would be so easy to just stay in bed and sleep for another few hours or just lie in bed reading. But this is the rocky road to lethargy and will not aide my recovery.

As a further discipline, I always clean out the fireplace and reset the fire ready for lighting in the late afternoon so the cottage is nice and warm for Sarah's home coming.

After this, I plan my day, allocating time to cover anything that needs to be done in the office on the computer for the flying school or forms, appointments and other requirements. I then do some work in the house or garden, as well as rest time. There are little jobs to be done in the garden and around the house. These are not very tasking, covering painting to small repairs.

As mentioned before I have discovered the joy of cooking and probably make some cakes & cookies about three times a week, which I give away as gifts, and then think about a meal for Sarah & I in the evening.

I keep my brain occupied by doing crossword puzzles, jigsaw's (the Cadbury Roses one is extremely difficult and took me six months to do!) or by playing games on the iPad. But the days still drag by and the highlight of the day is when Sarah comes home and we can have a nice hot bath and a drink before supper....and then relax and chat about our day.

I also go for a short walk through our lovely countryside – well its down the road, round to the church where I always stop to reflect on the forthcoming wedding; it's a beautiful church and a fantastic setting which fills me with hope and happiness; I then return back as I cannot manage to go far without getting exhausted, then I find it hard to walk. But I am determined to get rid of dear old 'sticky' before the wedding, so I need to start to learn how to walk using the stick purely as a prop. It's frustrating having the car outside and not being able to drive it ….. the temptation to jump in and go up the road is huge – but I resist!!

It's a funny thought when you look at my current situation – I own a flying school with two aircraft and a suspended pilots licence and my new car on the drive with a suspended driving licence, I am a bit like a boy in a chocolate factory – I can look but not try!!

After six weeks the stroke community team finish their duty of care and hand me over to the community nursing team, so I have had visits from both the physio team as well as the Speech &

Language teams.

However, the SALT teams are still very concerned by my continued problem with swallowing. After six months they would have expected my ability to swallow would have re-learnt by my brain, but I still have major issues here. So they recommend a specific scan to determine what is happening.

On January 8th we went to see the ENT specialists and have a video Fluoroscopy scan of my throat to determine what solution the experts can come up with to help me with my swallowing and my voice box.

The scan consists of taking a custard mixed with dye and swallowing this, whilst they watch what is happening on the scanning screen, and again the same with a dye covered banana to see how a solid performs.

They show me the video. It's quite clear that food is being trapped at the top of gullet that the throat muscles are unable to force down, as they have been damaged by the stroke. They show me a new technique in helping me swallow, which I use now.

The benefits office finally come up with an ongoing payment package based on both my Employment benefit as well as the Personal Independent Payment, so at least we now have some financial help with some of the bills at home as my income stream from work has now ceased.

February flies by being a short month, and I am getting into my routine and settling down to spending most of the days on my own now, incarcerated in our lovely cottage. My visits from friends and neighbors slowing down as I have worn them out!!

But we start to prepare for the wedding, finalizing the guests lists and the table plans. Amazingly everyone we invited to the wedding last year, which we had to postpone, have accepted and there are around 100 people coming to our special day.

Twenty-eight weeks after my stroke, my walking has come on tremendously, I still have the left side of my face frozen, which affects my swallowing and speech and the right side of my body, arm and leg, are also frozen, with little sensation, temperature gauge or pain threshold. My eyes are still hurting, with double vision when I don't use my glasses (which still has the prism attached to one lens to straighten my dodgy eye), and I still get tired very quickly as well. My walking is now ok at home, but out of the house I use my stick to steady myself, although my physio is teaching me to walk properly but still with the stick as a guide.

One of the greatest challenges I have at the moment is managing the boredom. I am starting to get a little depressed by the loneliness of each day. Sarah goes off to work at 8am and when she has gone I try and busy myself with household chores to help contribute something towards running the house including re-setting the fireplace, washing and ironing as well as planning the evening meal. But I do get very tired and spend most afternoons zombie like in front of the TV.

I have been counselled on fighting depression, and reading about strokes on the web sites – it's the one danger that people who have suffered from strokes fall into, and once depression takes hold it can take over your whole life. Climbing out of it can be arduous and takes a lot of personal self-motivation. My view is to avoid falling down that trap, and I am quite a self-motivated character with a fairly high determination once I set my mind to it.

I do feel those tentacles of depression trying to wrap themselves around my feet. I try not to show it to Sarah, but we have some intuitive friends and neighbors who can see my battle.

One of those is a good neighbor who has suggested that I look at part time voluntary work and as she also helps out at the local Arts & Heritage Centre, she has suggested I go along with her one day to take a look.

The following week, we go to the Arts & Heritage Centre and I meet Abigail Rich the Centre Manager, and she shows me around.

It's a charity run business reliant on voluntary workers, that has a thriving café and shop as its main income generator, but also includes the local library, arts & local heritage center as well. They are in need of marketing help, and I soon find myself signing up to work two days a week as their Marketing Manager (V).

My job is to design and produce all the marketing leaflets and adverting material for the many areas they are involved in, and it absorbs me.

Sometime later, I find out that Susan my neighbor became concerned at my state of mind, and started to talk to Abigail about the opportunity to get me involved. This was so kind of her, and within two months of starting my voluntary role, I am invited to join the Board of Directors as Voluntary Marketing Director.

The work I do for the center is all computer based

and it keeps me busy thinking about new ideas on marketing the offers the Centre has and organizing some of the events and trips they do. I am also involved in the Strategic Planning of the Centre and future development with the other members of the Board.

Its absorbing and between the administration of the Flying School and the marketing work at the Arts & Heritage Centre – I have no time to become depressed!

I have another review with Dr. Goels the Ophthalmic specialist about my eyes – which show that there is at long last some improvement in my eye sight. I go and see the Orthoptist who confirms that the new prism prescription is now close enough for an eye test that could result in my glasses being made specially for me – instead of the stick on prism I have been struggling with. This mean that I can then see if I meet the DVLA conditions and eye test to be able to re-apply for my driving license.

As Sarah is a Dispensing Optician we make an appointment at her works for the test, and two weeks later I have my new glasses and a test certificate that will pass DVLA standards. Next step towards driving again is an appointment with my GP together with the DVLA forms.

Finally, I go to the long awaited stroke review on 26th March to see if there is any change to the blood clot and tear in the veins!! I see a different consultant as mine is on holiday. He looks at my records briefly and assesses my weight, blood pressure and does a few tests on my vision. He looks at my hands and my walking and then back to my charts and case history.

I am nervous as he seems to be confused. This does not look good.

He explains that the last scan we had shown the blood clot lodged in my brain and confirms that this will not change.

He also tells me that there is no point in having another MRI scan to see it the clot has reduced or removed as it will not show any difference. He explains that I have a Lateral

Medullary syndrome and the paralysis on my left side may continue to improve as will the left side of my face, but in reality they don't know. Little is known about the type of stroke I have had – so they don't have a lot to go on. He wanted to discharge me there and then, but I felt that he was rushing me out – NHS cut backs is what came to mind, so I asked for another review in six months which he agreed to.

I leave despondent and Betty drives me home. Sarah gets in from work and I have a meal ready for her. We talk about the review and she tries to lift my spirits up by looking at all the positives.

Well at least I can look forward to seeing my GP and getting the driving license renewal under way.

I understand from the DVLA that as I had voluntarily surrendered my driving licence – I am able to re-instate myself on the condition that my GP is satisfied that I pass the DVLA health and eye sight requirements. So I go and see my GP.

He is very happy with both my health, my walking, my balance and my eye sight as we have the full test result from the opticians. So he signs the forms and I post them off, waiting in anticipation.

Sarah and I have also started to slowly and gently resume our intimate relationship and for me, it's another indication of my return to as normal a life as possible, it's also a very important side of our relationship.

From the beginning of April Sarah and I realize that it is not long until our wedding day, and we start to get busy with the final arrangements. Sarah takes a week off so we can meet with the photographer, the cake people, the florist, the hotel and reception, the room dresser and Sarah has more dress fittings.

The weather has again been fantastic, as per last year and we are enjoying a beautifully warm, sunny spring. I have mastered the stone steps up to the garden now and am able to sit either on the upper lawns in the back garden or on the lower patio. But the time has come to start to think about cutting the lawns. Last year after my stroke, friends and neighbors came to cut the grass for me, but this year I am determined to do this myself as part of my rehabilitation.

I am warned by everyone, especially Sarah about over exerting myself and I promise to take my time, with several breaks for a rest on one of the two bench seats in the garden.

It's a major achievement for me, and I look at it as walking practice as all you are doing in fact is holding onto the handle bars or the mover and propelling it in a more or less straight line!!

My very first attempt was a comedy of errors. Due to the stroke I tend to lean or drift to the right as I am left side dominant. So the lines on the lawn were curved in an 'S' shape. Sarah thought it was so funny that it added some artistic impressions to the look of our rear lawn.

Over the weeks I mastered the straight line, and my walking improved to boot!!

In May I get a letter from the DVLA and my licence renewed!! I can drive again!!

I cannot wait to try after nearly 11 months of not driving. So I sent Felix a text message to see if he is free – he only lives down the road and works largely from home. He agrees and within the hour he backs the CLK down the drive and we put the roof down as it's a lovely sunny day. He parks on the street and lets me into the driver's side. I adjust the seat, mirrors and familiarize myself with all the controls.

I am nervous and have that knot in the pit of my stomach when you are about to do something really exciting.

The ignition key turns and she fires up. The excitement in me bubbles over and I have to calm myself down. I select drive on the automatic gear box, and slowly depress the accelerator ...... and we are off!!

We decide to drive to the airport so that I can pick some papers up, and it's a 'B' road so little or no traffic. Felix is a bit concerned that I drive too much to the right and wants me to follow the road side on the left.

But it's totally exhilarating driving an open topped car like this. I love it. I don't go over 40 mph all the way there and back – it seems fast enough to me, and Felix is reasonably relaxed with my driving. It's a major event in my continued recovery as it now means that I have transport and can drive around locally for myself and not be reliant on so many people.

Its sheer freedom and feels really great!

This also means that I can go back to my regular Saturday morning swimming. For the last 23 years I have been swimming at 8am every Saturday morning, started when my daughters were young and went to the small pool to learn, so I joined the adult swimming course in the big pool.

It is very good exercise and we have a brilliant and attractive instructor, who puts us through our paces, varying the stroke each week. She pushes us to swim as many length as we can and as an ex county and competitive swimmer (in my youth) I am allocated to the 'fast' lane.

I used to swim 46 to 50 x25 meter lengths before the stroke but can only manage about 32 to 36 now.

The benefits are that there is a regular crowd and we have been swimming for many, many years together, and its good exercise and discipline; having to get up and leave home by 7.20am on a Saturday.

The first time I got into the pool, it had been 11 months since I last swam, so I was very nervous, not only because I didn't know if I could remember how to swim (well I can't ride a bike anymore!) and although the welcome back was very warm and genuine from everyone, our instructor was a bit worried and asked if I needed any help in the pool.

'Well Lisa, we shall soon find out!' I said as I jumped into the water.

Now please remember that the right side of my body has no temperature recognition, neither has the left side of my face; so the sensation on entering the water was indeed very weird. I could feel the water temperature on the left side of my body and right side of my face, but on the opposite side was nothing but a luke warm feeling!!

Next …… can I swim??

'Peter, why don't you gently try to do breast stroke first …. And please be careful' a very worried Lisa stood on the pool side ready to dive in after me.

I push off the wall and stretch out to a horizontal position and start to kick like a frog with my legs and then automatically my arms started to stretch forward and scoop water back in the traditional breast stroke. YES I CAN !! Hurrah.

I complete a length of the 25-meter pool slowly and decide to try front crawl on the way back.

This was interesting as my stroke favored my left side – so I tended to drift right. I cannot swim in a straight line, much to everyone's amusement.

I reach the pool end and Lisa our instructor asks me if I am ok, and not to tire myself out. I go another couple of lengths before I stop, as I take heed of what I am being told.

But this means that I can slowly return to full swimming, and all the doctors and specialists have told me it's the best form of exercise for my condition. A Bonus!!

Sarah

We are settling into a routine now and Peter Seems to be enjoying the new role of a 'house husband'. Every night I come home from a long day at work on my feet, to a Vodka & Tonic; a

lovely hot bath, and a delicious cooked meal, plus
Peter's efforts at baking whatever cakes, cookies or
puddings he has read in a magazine.
He is an avid reader of Delicious Magazine which
is all about cooking and comes up with some
amazing dishes, and a few not so amazing!! And he
is amassing quite a number of cook books as well –
which worries me!
Susan, one of our neighbors has approached me
regarding Peter's state of mind, and his boredom.
She is concerned that she sees him walking around
the village aimlessly and when she talks to Peter he
openly admits that he is bored.
Susan suggested that she could introduce him to
the local Arts & Heritage Centre where she does
voluntary work, as they are desperate for someone
to take charge of their marketing – which is right
up Peters street. I think it's a great idea, but it's got
to be seen as his decision to start working there.
Susan think she knows how to achieve this.
A week later I come home from work to a very
excited Peter. He is buzzing and it's so great to see
him so alive again. He is animated about how
much help they need and what he can do for them.
I am a little concerned that he will over extend
himself, because true to character,
Peter does things at 110 mph, and its all of nothing.
We just need to keep a small hand break on him to
keep him centered on what his is able to do and
not to overstretch his physical abilities.
Susan collects him every Tuesday and Wednesday
to take him to the Centre in Castre and brings him
home again. On occasions Abigail the Manager will
pop down to collect him.

He is so focused and motivated – it's just what he needed to help his recovery.

I know he gets very frustrated and despondent at some of the results he is receiving from his doctors, but the good news in April was that he could soon be driving again, and he gets his licence back in May.

This will make a massive difference to him, as lack of mobility is his biggest frustration. Being able to drive himself will open up his options and give him a freedom and independence that hopefully will contribute towards his continued recovery … not to mention his state of mind.

For me …. Well it's one more thing for me to worry about – him on the road in a car on his own!! Heaven forbid he gets his pilot's licence back ….. I will need sedatives to calm my nerves.

He is progressing well though when you look at where he has come from, and we are told that what he has achieved in the eight months or so since his stroke is remarkable. It's down to his sheer determination to get back to normal.

In May he starts to go swimming again and although he has been told its good for him, I still worry about the drive to Brydges, and how much he will push himself to get back to what he used to do.

So I put a call into the Leisure Centre to talk to the instructor about keeping her eye on him. I am amused that again, she tells me that Peter is bound to go at 100 mph, and we both laugh about it. But at least I know he will be kept in control.

I do worry about what will happen if he is told that he won't make a full 100% recovery, because I understand that with every stroke, especially as severe as he had, there will always be something left that stops him from making a full recovery.

So I go to work every morning and leave him to his own devises. I know he goes for a walk every day, but its only down through the fields and back – less than a mile at most. He cannot manage any further even with 'sticky' his trusted prop.

Everyone does still call him on the phone or mobile – if not in person, and although the OT teams have finished their obligations he is still under review with his swallowing and needs more tests.

I came home one day in early May to find that he had attempted to mow the lawn despite my insisting that we get someone else to cut it for the time being. But Peter's determination and bull-headedness just made him ignore me and he got the mower out and started to make an absolute mess of the lawn. I couldn't help but laugh at the mess he had created. The lines were all over the place …. None were straight and he missed big clumps of uncut grass everywhere!!! It was like a horticultural Picasso abstract.

Peter tells me that he wants to cut the lawn as it helps his recovery and strengthens his walking; I reluctantly agree on the condition that I am at home when he cuts the lawn.

I have every Friday off and most Sundays – so we always plan to go somewhere, even if it's to Thrunscoe to walk slowly along the promenade and have lunch nearby. Sometimes we pick mum up and go to Lowth or Larken or if we are feeling adventurous we go to Beverley or York for the day. It gets Peter out and more exercise than he realizes, when we stroll round the shops in York stopping frequently for coffee's or drinks.

I also know he is working hard on the wedding plans and it keeps him busy. His eye sight is improving every day now – which is a godsend. He has so far kept very motivated, and has avoided the dreaded depression, which we were warned about by the Occupational Therapists.

With the wedding plans, the work he does at the flying school and the Voluntary work at The Centre, Peter has a busy schedule which is what we want.

For my birthday in May, Anne invites us down together with mum and Jane for a week's holiday. It means that mum and my sister can meet Peter's family, well Anne's daughter and son and their families, and it gives Peter and I a break. Anne has a beautiful home and is always so generous a host. We take mum and Jane to Lands' End, spending a good couple of hours walking around the cliff tops, calling in on Penzance town center on the way.

We went to Padstow where the famous chef Rick Stein has a few restaurants, and had lunch in his most famous one.

Padstow itself is a very interesting town and had a lot of little boutique shops to look around.

Peter and Roy got bored though! The fish lunch was delicious. We also go to St Ives which mum especially liked as it was a stunning little town with loads of shops too.

I shared the driving down with Jane as we didn't want Peter to drive at all, so he sat in the back with mum on the 8-hour drive to Cornwall. We stopped several times on the way for coffee breaks and arrived at Anne's mid-afternoon.

Anne lives in a tiny sea side hamlet just south of Falmouth in a beautiful American style ranch house. Its huge, all on one level, except for Anne's bedroom suite which has been built into the roof space and covers the whole length of the house. There are five bedrooms down stairs, all off a long corridor, with a huge kitchen, sitting room and dining room. The views are stunning, as it overlooks the cove or inlet leading to the main river Tamar.

The house is stunning, and mum and Jane are well impressed.

Anne is also an excellent cook, consummate host and spoiled us all with delicious mouth-watering dishes, whilst we were there. The weather turned out to be a mixture of sunshine and showers, but that did not deter us from our planned trip. In addition to Lands' End, Padstow and St Ives there are also several National Trust gardens and houses down there and we explored all of them.

So rather than having a restful time, we were full on all week. I did most of the driving – although Anne took us around as well, and we took the train to St. Ives. It was all very enjoyable and mum and Jane especially enjoyed their first visit to Cornwall. The drive home took nine hours and when Jane drove Peter sat in the front to help her and give her confidence – she had never driven on long motorways like this before. Peter was visibly tired when we got home, and it took its toll and over two days to recover.

Chapter Five

The Wedding
June to September

Peter

Nineteen days to go!

Now getting quite excited too, as memories of last year invade my thoughts.

Nothing is going to happen this year ….. please!!

I have nineteen days to finally master walking unaided, without 'sticky', so I practice every day and walk around on my own concentrating on what I have been taught with my posture and concentrating on my balance.

We have a lot of planning to do. Although everything is paid for, we still have to confirm details and timing with all the suppliers, and go through the menu and hotel guest lists with the reception venue.

Everyone we have sent an invitation to has accepted – it's fantastic that all our friends will be there. Some of my pals I have known for over 30 years and they have all set aside their plans to be with us on our happy day. I am so elated, and Sarah knows how happy this makes me.

We have about 20 couples staying in several local hotels, and to enable our guests to relax and enjoy the day, we have organized a coach to collect them from their hotels to bring them to Rodewelle for the

service at 3pm and then take them all back with the local village friends to the venue, and return them to their hotels and Rodewelle at midnight. This seemed the best bet as parking in our village is limited, especially near the church and people can congregate at the local pub beforehand and walk up to the church – especially if it a nice day.
Note: place order for a nice sunny day!!
Mike – our Best Man and Paula have offered to drive us both after the wedding to the venue in his black Range Rover, and Roy has volunteered to collect the bridesmaids, Betty and Sarah from our cottage to the church, although it's only a three-minute walk.
I plan to stay with Mike and Paula on the evening before, but we also plan to meet at the pub with my sister and other friends who are staying local as well.
Sarah and I have meeting with the photographer, and then go to see the manager of the reception venue to go through the planned afternoon and evening.
The vicar or should we say Cannon, wants a dress rehearsal a week before the wedding and everyone comes, my best man, best usher, Sarah's sister and mum and we go through the ceremony. Sarah and get a reality check and it feels so good that we are finally going to get married after the last year.
The little church of St Mary Magdalene in Rodewelle is a Norman Church dating back to 11th and 12th Century, and is even listed in the Doomsday Book in 1086 as Rodewelle Church – so a very historic Grade 1 listed building, and is a very pretty church too. It holds about 100 people so it's

going to be cozy on the day. We have arranged to
have the grass cut 4 days before and the paths
swept. Sarah has ordered flower garlands for
outside and inside the church as well as
decorations and six olive trees in pots!!

As I lost so much weight – nearly three stone – my
planned wedding suit hangs off me, and so we all
plan a shopping trip to York, with Jane, Betty and
Sarah. I manage to buy off the peg a very nice navy
blue suit from TM Lewin and a shirt as well, and
Sarah chooses four pick ties for all of us to wear. I
still have no idea what her wedding dress is like,
but know that she had bought three, so what she
plans is beyond me!!

On the day before the wedding, all our chores were
done and we had a couple of hour's spare, so Mike
suggested we go flying, just around the Humber
Bridge and back, 40 minutes max.

As Mike is an instructor he told me I would fly in
the left hand seat, so he did external checks as I
busied myself in the familiar cockpit with internal
pre-flight checks. It was a beautiful sunny
afternoon and we took off and climbed up to two
thousand feet. As we approached the planned
height, I foolishly commented of the fact that I
hadn't forgotten how to fly as it was the first time
since we went to Carlisle, the day before the Stroke.
'Oh really, well let's see how much you have
forgotten' Mike said; and promptly pulled the
throttles shut. 'Engine failure, practice forced
landing' Mike said.

'Oh you shit' I responded, and went into
emergency mode as I had been trained and set the
aircraft up for a cruise descent and started to look

for an appropriate field to aim for a safe landing –
but this was only a practice so we would actually
land in the field!

During our training for our pilot's licence and
every six months we practice emergency
procedures that cover engine failure on take-off;
engine failure at altitude; engine fires, stalls and
other emergencies, so that if we actually find
ourselves in an emergency situation we are trained
to bring the aircraft down safely. This was one
exercise that we practice, so I went through all the
emergency checks in the cockpit whilst at the same
time, looking out for somewhere to land and flying
the plane with the propeller just ticking over!

'Which field Peter are you going into'

'That green one down there' I replied

'Ha ha that's really funny – they are all green, now
come on Peter, which field are we going into'

So I indicated the field I had selected into wind and
long enough to make a safe landing – if this was
real.

As we came over the fields hedge at 50 feet he
called 'Go around …. That was good …. you would
have made it in safely. Climb away'

So I gunned the throttle and retracted one stage of
flap and pulled back on the control column to
climb away back up to two thousand feet.

'Not bad Mr. Hall. You did OK after what ….
Nearly a year?'

We flew around the Humber Bridge and back to
the airfield and landed. Just as we were taxiing in
we saw that someone was waiting on the apron for
the aircraft as we had overrun into his time.

That was exhilarating and was just the tonic I

needed. I was grinning from ear to ear all night.
We went back to Mike's house to change and drive
with Paula to meet my sister and friends for dinner
at our local pub.

I woke up at seven to a beautiful day; it was warm
– and a mixture of high cloud and sunshine, just
what we wanted. If it was a blazing hot day,
everyone would be wearing sunglasses in the
sweltering heat, and all the pictures taken outside
would be spoiled. As it was it was warm and dry
but not glaringly bright, so the photographer was
very happy.

Our wedding day went by very quickly …. too fast,
which was a real pity, as it was the very best day of
my entire life. Mike and I and my best men got to
the church a good forty minutes early, and spent
some time outside the church greeting people as
they arrived.

Then with twenty minutes to go I was taken inside
by Mike and told to wait at the chancel. I was so
nervous, Mike stood next to me and I think was as
nervous as I was. Sarah was traditionally late in
arriving, so the wait was quite long. The church
was packed to maximum, with all our friends and
family, some had to sit in the choir stalls in the
chancel itself; the atmosphere was electric and
buzzing as everyone were very excited for us.

When the vicar nodded to the organist to start
Mendelsohn's Wedding March, Mike whispered in
my ear.

'Don't look round Peter, its bad luck'

Then as Sarah started to walk up the central aisle
through the nave, he said out loud:

'My god she looks stunning, don't look round ….

Peter no you mustn't'
But the temptation was far too great and I had a
quick look.
Sarah looked breathtakingly beautiful when she
walked very slowly up the aisle with Betty her
mum. She came and stood next to me and I had to
catch my breath. She was stunning …. No other
words, she took my breath away.
The church was packed with standing room only,
and when we sang the hymns everyone raised their
voices so that the roof shook its timbers with music.
I did not have 'sticky' with me, he was in the car. I
managed to walk on my own, up to the altar for the
blessing and to sign the register and I walked my
beautiful bride down the aisle without a problem.
But she was gripping me quite tightly on my arm
to steady me!
On the drive back to the reception venue Mike and
Paula had a chilled bottle of Champagne for us to
enjoy and Mike had his Range Rover gleaming
with cream ribbons on the door handles.
We reached the venue before the coach arrived and
some guests were there already along with the
photographer. He took Sarah and I to the gardens
and lake for photographs before we joined our
friends and family in the courtyard for prosecco
and canapes.
The wedding breakfast started at 6pm, in the barn
shaped main dining hall of the venue, which Sarah
had very skillfully decorated each table in white
silks.
I made all the table name cards and menu lists, and
we had favors for the ladies and lottery tickets for
the men. The meal was delicious as we had

expected from the restaurants reputation, and the speeches excellent.

We did not stick to tradition as both our fathers were deceased, and Betty didn't feel confident enough to stand in front of a hundred people to say a few words. So my sister volunteered to speak on behalf of the family and some very kind words about Sarah and some hilarious anecdotes about me.

She was very good and had the guests in laughter. I stood up this written speech that I had rehearsed a thousand times, but found difficult to project my voice or see the words as I was so emotional.

Anne, my sister started the speeches with a very good tale of her little brother and her new sister-in-law. She was brilliant.

I am next with my speech: I am very nervous.

Thanks Anne for those kind words.....

Good evening everyone, and on behalf of my wife and I, a very warm welcome to our special wedding day ......at long last!

Well - as promised in our new-invitations - I did behave myself and I am on cloud 10! The happiest man on earth. I know this sounds unusual... But I must start with some apologies....

Apologies to everyone here for spoiling a good party last July ..... a bit of a drastic way to get cold feet I know but..... only kidding!!

Apologies to all the ladies in the room for the additional expense of having to buy new outfits for your husbands, boyfriends or other halves! .... (pause) .....No....I think I've got that the wrong way round!!

Apologies for not having another stag do ....but the

BOSS put her foot down!
And apologies to the BOSS, – my Sarah ....I am so sorry for giving you such a scare last year and I promise to concentrate on getting back to full health.
You know Sarah is so brilliant, ...whilst I was in hospital she used to breeze in during visiting hours and greet all my fellow inmates with a cheery smile and a wave ....and they used to say...."here comes the lovely bride" ...and it made me laugh so much and it also made me so proud as well…..and got me through those initial 3 weeks.
By the way guy's – good luck with the lottery tickets tonight….if you win, we are Peter & Sarah Hall and our number is 07880-0888999!!!
Now a few thank you's.....
Thank you Betty for making me feel so welcomed into your warm and loving family. I would have loved to have met Sarah's Dad, Henry – who is sadly no longer with us…..he would have been so proud of his beautiful daughter today. (flowers presented to Jenny)
Thank you to Matthew, Stacey and the team here at the venue for agreeing to postpone the wedding date to today and for laying on such an enjoyable meal.
I would like to thank my ushers Paul and my new brother in law Andrew, for helping with crowd control and getting you all safely into the church and out to Hall Farm.
And finally I would like to thank my new sister –in- law Jane and my new Niece-In-Law Poppy for looking after my gorgeous Sarah, for supporting her in the build up to this our fantastic day and for agreeing to be maid of honor and bridesmaid.
I have to say that the last 11 months have been the scariest in my life and I don't want to experience that again.

Just to remind you that Sarah was rushed into hospital 8 weeks before our planned wedding last year with kidney stones, then I had my stroke 11 days before hand. Well what a year!!

Everyone in this room today are very special to both Sarah and I and it's with a huge heartfelt thanks to all of you for your help and support to Sarah and to me especially, throughout my recovery from the stroke. You have all in one way or another been instrumental in my mental approach to overcoming and conquering this illness. So thank you!

Sarah and I are thrilled that you, our closest friends and family, have come to witness our marriage and help us to celebrate today, and it's amazing that virtually all of you have been able to re schedule your diaries to be here this year.

Since moving to Rodewelle, Sarah and I have made some brilliant new friends....that's the wild rowdy lot up there in the gallery.   Welcome to you all - fellow Rodewellians!!

*We have virtually all of our best Friends here today ....
Sarah's friends I have had the great pleasure of meeting and am getting to know, and my very special friends, some of you I have known for over 30 years.*

I would like to say a special thanks to Vita for the reading in church and to Roy, both have been there for Sarah & I through some difficult times over the past 4 years and have been very supportive, especially with their very wise advice.

And a massive thanks to Paul & Libby. Both of these fabulous people have helped us so much in so many ways and the greatest news we had last month was that they got engaged in New Orleans and are planning the happy day soon...so another party...congratulations!!

I would like to make a very special mention to my oldest and dearest friend Jose, whom I have known since I was 18 – so that's over 45 years. We are godfathers to our respective eldest daughters, he is like my older brother and he is now my only link to my home land in Peru. Very sadly my mum and dad are no longer with us, but my big sister Anne is here with Charles. Anne and I both know that Mum especially would have loved Sarah. So Sarah on behalf of Anne and I welcome to our family!!

And finally, I want to thank my best man Mike for all his solid friendship and support, his very wise counselling and guidance throughout the last 24 years, but most especially this last year where he and Paula have always been here for Sarah & I - throughout my recovery.

Mike phones me every week wherever he is around Europe to see how I am and probably comes to see me every other week as well, to make sure Sarah and I are ok and to help wherever he can.

It's also a bit of a role reversal actually because I was privileged to have been his best man when he married the gorgeous Paula 9 years ago.

I asked Mike to be my best man quite some time ago. In fact I proposed to Sarah in their kitchen …..yes I am a very romantic man ….and asked Mike to be my best man at the same time.

Some of you will know Mike, but for those that don't, he is an exceptionally talented pilot, ex RAF fast jets, a commercial captain with over 17000 hours of flying experience, and now he fly's the rich and famous around in private jets.

I have been reliably informed that Mike has been very nervousness about his best man's speech and it is rumored that for the last year he has built a reputation amongst his fellow flight deck crew.

Picture the scene: he is on the runway in Nice bound for Moscow with some billionaire magnate or super star in the back......, gets clearance to take off, thrust leavers forward, accelerates down the runway, pulls back on the control column, gets airborne, calls to first officer "positive rate of climb, wheels up, flaps up, auto pilot on ....and then reaches for his best man's speech.

Apparently there is an email going round InterJet from all the co-pilots that they should avoid flying with Mike until after 19th June.

Seriously though ...Mike & Paula ....thank you both for your huge support, most especially over this last year.

  Right ....here is a challenge to all the men....and ladies if you like ale. We have specially ordered in a barrel of Tom Woods Best Bitter and the restaurant here have never sold a whole barrel before at a wedding. I have to pay for any beer that is left.....so the challenge is....can we drink it all and enter the Hall Farm record books as the first wedding to clear a barrel of beer....it will save me eating into my pension too!!!!!

Pause......

And now to my gorgeous bride. Doesn't she look stunning!!

I met Sarah at The Opticians 10 years ago and I fell in love with her.....it was a prescription made to last!! ......oh god ...Excuse the opticians pun!!

Well she apparently also felt the same way about me.....there was something very magical ....a magnetic pull, and I knew then that she would eventually become part of my life.

I am indeed a very lucky man, to have met this incredible lady. She is gorgeous, witty, intelligent, and brilliant at her job (both her bosses are her so I had to say that!) and the most incredible fact is that we are so compatible in every aspects of our lives.

We like the same things, we even think about the same things...often know what the other is about to say and we are so comfortable and easy in each other's company...

a true sign of compatibility...and all my friends and my family love her too.

We have been living together for 4 years and in that time my whole life has changed for the better, despite the stroke.

I think you will agree that she really showed her true colours in July last year, when she had to step up and take over my whole life....dealing with everything....from my consultancy business, the flying school, the finances and handling all the contacts with friends and family...and at the same time, coming to see me in hospital....and of course doing her own job too....an incredible lady.

And I would like to say a huge thanks to June and Gordon, her bosses, for being so supportive towards Sarah and I during those very difficult months last year.

Honey.....the pressure and stress you were under during those months was phenomenal and you really must love me so much to have been through all that. It makes me love you so much more for it too...you are truly my rock.

I have never been as happy as I have been since I met you, so thank you for coming into my life, for sticking by me and supporting me throughout my illness and most of all, for finally becoming my wife.

I promise to keep on getting better, to behave myself so we have a long term future together, and to support you in any way I can.......being the very best house husband ever!

I love you so very much Mrs. Hall..

*And so, our friends and families, it falls on me to please
ask you to be upstanding and raise your glasses to the
matron of honor and bridesmaid.*
A toast to Jane and Poppy.
…….. it was a well-received groom's speech.
 Mike, my Best Man, was absolutely brilliant, with
a very well written speech that was backed up by
pictures of me in my youth as well as Sarah and he
had the whole room in stitches of laughter. He also
managed to make fun out of my stroke, which was
hilarious. And the pictures of both of us
as toddlers he had must have been supplied by
Anne and Betty. It was the highlight of the night
and I was in awe of Mike.
We were cutting the cake by 9pm and the singer we
hired started with the first dance. So by ten pm I
was absolutely shattered, and had to go to our
room to have thirty minutes' rest, as Sarah got
changed into her evening wedding dress. So that
was the second dress, but what was the third?
We re-joined our guests down stairs, with those
who had noticed our disappearance and Sarah's
change of dresses with a knowing wink or remark
about being impatient to 'cement' the marriage!
Little did they know that it was the stroke that tired
me out.
We danced and talked to everyone for the rest of
the night which seemed to speed through on a fast
forward button as no sooner than we realized it
was midnight and the coach and cars had arrived
to take everyone home or to their hotels and we
finally went to bed …… and did make love for the
first time as man and wife.
'Sticky' stayed in the room all night!!

Sarah

Nineteen days to go, and we have loads to organize for the wedding.

Peter has made all the table place names, the table menu cards, the table plan which we are having framed in a huge white mirror frame, and bought the lottery tickets as favors for the men.

I have got several fittings for my dress and go with Jane and ……..to see their dresses too as they are bridesmaids. I must admit to buying three dresses. Well the first one I bought I ended up not liking and after Peters stroke, mum and Jane came with me to the wedding dress shop and saw this second dress which we thought would be great to change into for the evening. Then I tried on this stunning third dress and fell in love with it.

It was in a champagne colour and had one shoulder bare, and it was very slender and long with a small train.

But the material and cut of the dress made me look stunning, and all I wanted was to be perfect for Peter. They suggested how my hair should be and my hairdresser came and saw me in the dress as well so he could get a visual idea of what we wanted.

I was very nervous as I know Peter kept hinting at what the dress was like, but we teased him with totally different descriptions he got confused.

As it was – on the day- he just gawped at me, unbelievably and was overwhelmed by the beauty of the dress and how I looked.

It was perfect.

Peter and I also visit the room planners and designers, who will dress the tables and chairs and decided on a theme. I was very happy with our decision.

We had to have several meetings with the reception venue and the photographer and Peter ordered a second fruit based cake from a good friend of his who has started a cake business, as an alternative to the original sponge one we had ordered for our aborted wedding.

Our wedding day was going to be perfect and everyone invited had accepted so we had a full house.

The dress rehearsal at the church with the Cannon went very well and brought home the reality that we were finally getting married. Mum and I dressed the church with flowers and olive trees and it looked stunning.

Our plan was that I would stay at home with Jane on the evening before and mum and my best friend Suzi came for drinks. We had all morning until 2.45pm to get ready, so my hair dresser, beautician and dress maker all came to the house to help us get ready. Mum had bought a stunning silver dress and she looked lovely, and we all enjoyed being pampered whist sipping Prosecco that Peter had chilled for us.

I spoke to Peter earlier that morning to make sure that he and Mike put out the table name cards correctly and placed the ladies and men's favors out as well. He told me he and Mike had done that the day before then they had gone flying ...... of all things only they could do!! Well I am glad I didn't know yesterday otherwise I would have been panicking!!

The weather turned out to be just right, it was warm, with a mixture of high cloud and glimpses of sun light which meant that it was not glaring enough for dark glasses. Thinking of the pictures. I originally planned to walk to the church as it was just down the road and up through a small wooded path next to the main field, but Roy offered to collect us in his new silver Mercedes and drive us round the long way …. All of one minute!!

Jane and Polly went first and Roy came back for me and mum.

The excitement grew like a fire in my belly as the final realization hit me that we had actually, finally made it to our wedding. As we arrived at the church main entrance the photographer was there snapping away as mum and I made our way down the graveled path through the headstones of the 11th century Norman cemetery that surrounded the church.

The Reverend Cannon met us at the door, and asked me if I was ready.

'Yes please' I stammered

My heart was racing and I was flush with excitement. I worried about how I looked and couldn't wait to see Peters face at the altar.

This was it.

My actual wedding!

Mum held onto me as we started to walk very slowly up the aisle, I wanted this to take its time and I savored every step I took. It was the best time of my whole life.

We had come so far since I nearly lost the love of my life. I never thought Peter would make such a good recovery, to be able to be here today, standing there looking so distinguished and smart …. And without his stick too.

My heart just overflowed with so much emotion and love when he looked at me and said
'You are beautiful, absolutely stunning …… is it really you?' then added as a whisper in my ear
'God I love you'

And so we got married and Peter walked me down the aisle as Mrs. Hall without 'sticky' and into the grounds of the little church for the confetti run and more pictures.

It was a perfect day!

Mike and Paula had a bottle of champagne for us to drink on the way to the reception venue and I held on to Peter in a daze. When we arrived the photographer took us straight to the lakes behind the venue for special photos and then we re-joined our friends for the canapes and cocktails in the courtyard.

During the speeches Peter said some lovely words to me – they were very emotional. Anne and Mike also made very funny speeches and all of our friends were in stitches of laughter.

I was worried about Peter towards the end of the wedding breakfast and as we cut the cake as he seemed unsteady on his feet. I took him off as soon as the first dance was over and took him to our room for a brief rest, as I changed into my evening wedding dress.

He had a thirty-minute rest and slept, so he was fresher when he woke up. He dressed down into just his shirt and trousers and we re-joined our guests for the rest of the evening.

At nine-thirty the venue brought out a cheese buffet which was huge, but everyone dug in and had some.

We danced to the singer and DJ for the rest of the night ….

It was just such a perfect day.

Peter – Honeymoon

We did not depart for our honeymoon until the Monday morning, which enabled us to spend Saturday night with Anne and Charles, our close family and friends. Anne and Charles were heading off back to Cornwall early doors on Sunday so it was nice to spend some time with them.

We had originally booked a week in Sorrento, before I had the stroke, but as I am not allowed to fly, we changed our plans to stay in a bijou boutique hotel on the North Norfolk coast

We had a very pleasant casual drive down – and as some were on 'B' roads and the weather was fantastic, we put the roof down, and arrived mid-afternoon. It was in a lovely setting. But thank god for Satnav otherwise we would not have found it.

It had individual cottages in the grounds of a country house, each were unique and individual with all the required features.

Ours boasted a giant double king size bed, with a sitting area, and a huge bath, big enough for four people to sit in, and a glorious walk in rain shower. The room was extremely well appointed and no expense spared on the luxury and quality of the

furniture. It will be our base for the next week as
we go exploring the North Norfolk coast.

The hotel boasted an A La Carte meals cooked by
the owner – a professional chef – on a dinner, bed
& breakfast basis – the breakfast choices were
abundant every morning and you had your own
table. They only had one sitting for dinner so
everyone was served cocktails or drinks with
canapes at 6.45, followed by dinner, which
comprised of a menu choice from 5 dishes, all
freshly cooked by the chef. Their wine selection
was all high quality and the evening meal consisted
of three courses plus a cheese board every night.
We both put on a stone in weight, but hell …. It
was our honeymoon, so we didn't care.

For most lunches we only had a light snack,
knowing what was coming that evening. Only on
one lunch time – we were recommended to go to a
fish restaurant on the beach near Cromer for a cold
sea food platter. It was Sarah's introduction to
lobster and some other shell fish…. but all the
seafood they served was simply delicious,
including the world famous Cromer Crab.

The hotel complex had an indoor swimming pool
and Spa in grounds that covered several acres and
it was a most romantic setting, we had seen in a
long time.

Sarah and I had a fantastic honeymoon – driving
everyday with the roof down visiting castles,
stately houses, garden, towns and beeches.

Every day was warm and sunny. We did not rush,
took our time with everything and left our watches
in the hotel room so we had no concept of time.
It was magical and the most enjoyable time we

could have spent together.

Coming home at the end of the week was not an anti-climax as Sarah still had several days off work to spend at home with me, so the honeymoon continued once we got home.

Sarah – Honeymoon

Peter was so excited about the boutique hotel he found on line on the North Norfolk coast near to Cromer. He wanted to drive, but I insisted on sharing the driving – well it was only a 3-hour leisurely drive stopping en-route for coffee and cakes.

It was a fabulous day on Monday and we spent most of the drive with the roof down, which made Peter drive slowly.

When we arrived at the hotel, we were stunned at the beauty of the setting and the very friendly greeting we received on arrival by the owners was un-expected. Our 'cottage' in the grounds was simply wonderful and it made me so happy. Peter certainly did very well in finding this hotel.

Later we discovered the sumptuous and delicious food, very personal service and excellent organization.

We 'dressed' for dinner every night, having cocktails and canapes before dinner.

In-fact the food was so good – we looked forward to our evening meal every day, so skimped on lunch.

Cromer is famous for its crab and the owner of the hotel suggested we went to this beachside seafood restaurant, run by the same family for over 100 years. The menu had never changed and we had the seafood special, and the first time I had ever tried lobster. It was delicious and don't know why I never tried it before.

We simply loved it. The pool we had all to ourselves and the communal dining with all the other hotel guests was a welcomed departure from the normal as it got us talking to some very interesting people.

Each day we put the roof down on the CLK and looked at the map to decide where we were going, and it's fair to say that we went to every stately home, castle, gardens in the area, as well as visiting interesting towns such as Holt and Cromer, and a few beaches.

I have to say that Peter and I both love this type of holiday, exploring castles, gardens and stately homes and just spending time sitting on a beach at Wells-next-the-Sea reading a book, just knowing we were there together. We had special treats of ice creams at Holkham Hall, built in 1730 by Thomas Coke the 1st Earl of Leicester and has been in the Coke family to this day where Thomas Edward Coke the 8th Earl of Leicester and his family live;, freshly fried doughnuts on Cromer Pier; posh Tea and delicious cakes at the beautiful Jacobean Blickling Hall in Aylesham, where it is said to be haunted by the ghost of Anne Boleyn, who was reputedly born on the estate; fish & chips out of newspapers at Blakeney village and seafood lunch at Cley. So we did spoil ourselves on honeymoon and put a good stone in weight on to boot!

We even took a steam train from Cromer to Holt.

When we got to Holt we caught the bus into town and found it was a lovely place with lots of little boutique shops which I enjoyed. Peter bought me a dress in one shop which I liked.

The steam train brought back memories for Peter in his early years when he first arrived in the UK and took the train to Cheltenham, it was a similar carriage to the one we were in. I could see by the dark shadow across his face that he was re-counting in his mind those days that he didn't particularly like. But it was an adventure albeit only thirty minutes or so.

On the last day we went home via Sandringham, having been here five years before. Her Majesty was out at the time – so no invitation to tea, but we did the tour of the Palace and spent a good few hours wondering around the grounds, the little church and the museums they have there. It's a beautiful setting and one can just imagine what it's like for the Royal Family to get together here at Christmas.

It was a perfect honeymoon, and in retrospect, it was better than our original plans to spend time in Sorrento.

When we eventually got home, we still had a couple more days together as I had booked time off work to thoroughly enjoy the start of our new life together. So we pottered around at home, looking at all the wonderful and generous wedding gifts from all our friends and starting to send thank you cards to everyone.

Then – all too soon – it was back to the grindstone and the routine of getting up to go to work.

But I come home to my loving husband, who

always had a hot bath, a vodka & tonic and a delicious meal ready every night, bless him.

Peter – back home

What a fantastic wedding and honeymoon!
We could not have asked for a better time; the build-up to the wedding; the wedding day and the honeymoon; all planned meticulously and it all went without a hitch. I suppose you can say that we had the opportunity to fine tune the original plans made a year earlier, and that is what made it so perfect and relaxed.
The only criticism we can say is that it all went far too quickly. I wish we could have set a slow motion mode on the day and made it go at quarter speed so that we could have cherished every second of the day. Sarah looked stunningly beautiful and I fell in love with her all over again.
When we arrived home, with Sarah being still off work, we both spent quality time opening all our very generous wedding gifts from our superb friends. We were thoroughly spoiled.
Sarah has to go back to work after nearly three weeks off, and I have to adjust to my new life as a 'house husband'. So I settle into a routine.
I always get up with Sarah, and get shaved, showered and changed. It's an important discipline. I always make her breakfast which we have together, before she goes to work. Then I get on with whatever I have planned for that day.
July, August and September are very hot months and between the Arts & Heritage Centre voluntary

work and the flying school (also voluntary) I have a little time to potter around the garden and the house and avoid become morose!!

In the garden I am restricted by The Boss as to what I am allowed to do. Weeding is on the NO list as I can't tell the difference between a weed and a plant; pruning is on the NO list as I cut the wrong branches; so I am allowed to mow the lawn and trim the edges, sweep up leaves and dispose of the garden waste.

But there is still plenty to do with cleaning the patio and paths, fences to fix and bird feeders to fill ….. all within my allowed capabilities!!

I still get very weary or exhausted from around 3pm every day and so spend this time sitting on our patio, or on the bench seat in the top garden, reading a book or writing this missive.

Occasionally I get a visit from friends, or Sarah's family, but the health teams have all signed me off and I have finished with the SALT team as the video fluoroscopy scan's showed that the damage to my throat muscles could not be repaired, and I had to work on perfecting my new swallowing technique. So basically the message was 'just get on with it'!!

The new big challenge for both Sarah and I is to lose all the weight we put on during our honeymoon!!

From a health perspective, I feel little has changed. I still have an issue with my swallowing, the paralysis of the left side of my face and my right side of my torso is still as it was with little or no change. My walking is OK but I have gone back to using 'Sticky' for support, as it has not improved to the extent that I can walk normally. My vision has been corrected as long as I wear my glasses, as soon as I take them off, everything goes double, and it makes me disorientated and dizzy. So a simple task like taking a shower is complicated by having to hold onto everything to stop me falling over.

Am I expecting too much?

I have a major stroke review coming up in October with the specialists, but I am still popping 12 pills a day, and I don't feel I have made any significant improvement towards being 100% recovered.

I have a lot of questions to ask – top of the list is the BIG one:

Will I make a 100% recovery and if so by when? And …….. If I will not, what will I be left with or is this it – how I am now?

Yes – I am frustrated.

Yes – I am impatient

Yes- I am expecting too much!!

Why? ….. well it's my body, my brain, my life; and my ambition is to beat this stroke and make a full recovery. I have to fight this!!!

I am 61 now – so still relatively young in today's age; I certainly don't look 61 and I don't feel or act like a 61-year old; I have a beautiful younger wife and the chance of personal happiness in my twilight years with someone I want to be with, but I did not bargain on the stroke and its remanence.

It is becoming more evident that I am unlikely to able to hold down a full time job or resurrect my consultancy company, as going back to that level of pressure and stress was not wise, and the requirement to drive such high mileage to do the job around the country would be a massive barrier.

I enjoy the voluntary work at the Centre and the
flying school was always going to be my retirement
hobby. So early semi-retirement looks very much
on the cards.
I am claiming benefits for both Employment
Allowance and Personal Independence Payments
and although I am totally entitled to these
payments as I am a fully paid up member of society
having contributed taxes as a higher rate payer
being a higher earner all my working life, I still feel
uneasy accepting these payments – but not guilty.
Besides Sarah and I need the income as her salary
alone will not cover the bills.
My friends and all the experts tell me I am entitled
to it so just accept it.
Poor Sarah, I must be a nightmare to live with at
the moment.

Sarah – back home

Our honeymoon was an absolute dream come true.
Peter has excelled himself in finding and booking
the hotel. It was simply better than I could ever
imagine.
Peter and I spent some real quality time together on
our honeymoon, and it was magical.
I booked extra time off so that there was no rush to
get back to work. It meant that we had time to open
and enjoy all the very generous gifts that all our
lovely friends bought us.
I eventually have to face the fact that the wedding
is over and it's time to face reality and go back to
work. The weather is still lovely so Peter can spend

sometime in the garden.

But I have to lay down some rules.

He is useless as a gardener as he clearly has no idea about the difference between weeds or plants and on the rare occasion that he has tried to help in the garden I have ended up having to replant perfectly good flowers, that he took for weeds!

On another occasion I returned from work to find that the front hedge has been trimmed, only ....all the greenery that was growing along the base, which were flowers that were yet to bud, had also been neatly trimmed away! Much to my annoyance!!

His lines have improved with the mower – so at least that was something. And he couldn't do much harm with a grass edger. Or so I think!

So – the rules are simple; he is only allowed to mow, edge and clean the patio and paths.

Oh, no, no, no -please don't get me wrong .... I am not going to become one of those harridan wives, laying down rules!!

Only this one little rule, as I do love my garden as much as I love Peter!

I am getting a little bit worried about Peter's state of mind, as he seems to be on the edge of obsession about making a full recovery. He is determined to be back to normal, but deep down, I don't think that is going to happen. He has a major stroke review coming up in October and this will be an important meeting where he will find out what future he will have.

Peter has had a few recent disappointments – for instance his video fluoroscopy scan showed the permanent damage to his throat, and the knock on effect of his swallowing. He still has issues with his walking, his eye sight and his dizzy spells – plus he gets very tired in the afternoons.

There is one thing I love about this man, is his determination at anything he does. He might be like a whirlwind at times but he has immense self-motivation and his cup is always half full, not half empty.

We will get through this – eventually, but this next stroke review will be the one where he will need my total support.

Fortunately, July, August and September turned out to be mostly days of balmy warm weather, similar to last year when Peter had his stroke.

We celebrate his first year by having his closest friend around for supper and Peter delights in preparing and cooking most of it himself to show how far he had come.

He is still heavily reliant on strong medication to control his blood thinning and pressure, his diabetes and cholesterol and as such he cannot drink that much, but it doesn't stop him enjoying the odd glass of prosecco or wine with the meal.

He does get very tipsy on very little now, which is slightly amusing as he used to drink like a fish and not be affected at all.

He also still tires easily so takes himself off to bed for forty winks, and comes back down refreshed.

He just loves entertaining and has a great group of close knit friends.

Chapter Six

October to December

Peter – October Review 16 months later

I have a major six monthly review with the stoke consultant at 2pm at Skidforth Stroke Unit. Mr. Khan, the Consultant is new, well new to me, as Mr. Sidra has gone to a stroke unit in India. The new consultant has studied my file and in fact had joined the stroke unit as I was leaving the hospital, so he had been made aware of my case as it was quite a rare stroke. I ask him to be very straight with me in terms of my on-going recovery.

'It's been fifteen months since the stroke and I would like a straight and honest opinion of my on-going recovery. I still have very little feeling on my right side of my body, no pain or temperature feeling; the left side of my face is still frozen, and I still get very tired – especially after three pm and I often get the dizzy spells after a little exercise or in the evenings' I start the conversation.

The Consultant turned to look at me directly and said in a very straight – matter of fact voice:

'Mr. Hall, I think you should come to terms with your condition and start to learn to live with what you have.

The partial paralysis you have is called 'Wallenberg

Syndrome' or some know it as 'lateral medullary syndrome'. This will be with you permanently for the rest of your life. It will never improve, nor will we be able to remove the blood clot that caused the stroke in the first place. This blood clot is in your medulla, and it is unlikely that it will clear. We cannot operate to remove it as it is so close to your spinal cord. The dizzy spells you get are caused by the blood vessels using other routes to bypass the clot'

'Wow, this is hard to take in. Will these dizzy spells and my tiredness ever improve?'

'How can I better explain it. Mmm .... It's like an accident on a motorway blocking a carriageway. The traffic uses all the side roads to bypass the accident and re-join the motorway at the next junction. Like this example, your blood is using all the millions of tiny vessels to bypass the clot to feed your brain and it is the pressure that this is causing that makes you dizzy or tired at times. There is no way round it'

'What about an operation to remove the clot – would that be feasible'

'As I said earlier Mr. Hall, we have ruled out any surgical procedures, as the proximity to your spinal cord and the location of the clot makes this an extremely risky operation, and we would not be prepared to consider it. You must understand that by now the section of the vein where the blood clot is stuck now resembles a dried pasta tube as it has lost all its life composition, and so it is very unlikely that the clot will now move' He was very matter of fact about it and the way he phrased it, was a final statement.

'What about the drugs I take, will these be reduced?'

'No I am afraid they won't for your own safety and wellbeing. As long as you continue to take the medication we prescribe, we can confidently say that you are unlikely to suffer a heart attack or another stroke. But you must keep taking them, as well as having regular blood screening and health reviews. You also need to keep your weight in check and need to lose a stone at least'

I sat in silence for a few moments taking it all in. He sensed my hesitation.

'Mr. Hall, the stroke you have suffered was very severe and you have made a remarkable recovery. Your determination, your willpower and your positive attitude has all contributed toward this recovery. You have made about an 70% recovery, but what you are left with is manageable if you learn to live with it. You need to adjust your lifestyle to cope with your condition, and seeing what you have achieved so far, I have no doubt in my mind that you will succeed. So basically ...... you need to just get on with it ...... and enjoy the life you have'

We talked about his willingness to continue to see me each six months to monitor my health and just to check that my condition does not deteriorate.

It was the first time anyone had been straight with me, and I did appreciate his directness, as well as his professional analysis of my condition.

I thanked him very much and he could see how much I needed to take on board. We shook hands and he said he would see me again in April.

As I walked out of his office I bump into some of

the OT team that helped me in the first three weeks in hospital and they were very impressed with the confidence in my walking and stance.

The drive home was somber as I reflected on what I had been told. On the one hand I was glad he was honest and open with me, but on the other hand it's quite a brutal reality to comprehend.

I phone Betty to talk to her about the results and she listens to me and reassures me that all will be ok. I also tried to call my sister but she was out playing golf. I sent Sarah a text message as I knew she would be busy at work, but just said all was well and would see her tonight.

Sarah was not due home until after six so I would have to wait to tell her all about my discussions with the consultant.

When I arrived home, I made a mug of tea and took it into the garden, sitting on the bench seat in the sunshine. It gives me time to reflect on the options I have open to me for my future.

I have just married the love of my life and due to the stroke, it's unlikely I am going to return to meaningful employment. According to the specialist I am going to have to get to grips with the changes I am going to have to adapt to live with the damaged elements of my body. The paralysis down my right side of my body and the left side of my face; the issue with swallowing, my eye sight, the dizzy spells and tiredness and the limits on my walking, my ability to drive any distance and my ability to give the required concentration, stamina and focus to work in commercial life again. I suppose I should be grateful that am very lucky this is all I have to cope with, as it could have been

very different and much worse. In hospital I saw
fellow in-mates who had different types of strokes,
that left them without the use of their limbs or
hands, or it affected their brains, speech and
rational thinking.

You see great men such as Andrew Marr, the TV
presenter and political broadcaster who suffered a
stroke in January 2013 that left him with paralysis
on his left side, although I am not sure about the
severity of the stroke or where it happened in his
brain. He has been fortunate to get back on his feet
and back to the rigors and pressure of public
Television within nine months. He is a beacon of
hope to all stroke victims and I for one look up to
him in awe.

I am also a very lucky man as Sarah has stood by
me, and will help me re-adjust to the new life. Her
love is unconditional to accept me for what I have
now become.

My will is strong and I am not a natural depressive.
Yes – I have had and will have times when my
resolve will wilt, and I may descend into the dark
side, but I am lucky that my fabric is one of a
positive mental disposition and I always look on
the up side of every situation.

I will adjust.

I will get through this.

I will lead as normal a life as possible.

Sarah arrives home and gives me a big hug,
holding onto me as she is aware of the bluntness of
the consultant's words having spoken to Betty, her
mum, before arriving home.

'I think we should talk about everything Mr. Khan
has told you, and work through this'

She whispers in my ear as she kisses me.

Sarah – Peters Stroke Review

This particular morning Peter is due to meet his
stroke consultant at the hospital for his six-month
review. He is nervous I can tell, as he is slightly
subdued.

I have to go to work but wish I could go with him
to be there to support him. I suggest that he asks
Mike, Paul or Vita to go with him, but he wants to
face this alone.

All day at work I cannot concentrate as I keep clock
watching knowing he has the meeting at one
o'clock. All afternoon I keep wondering how he is
and what the outcome is, but have a feeling deep
down, which I have had for some time, that he has
made as full a recovery as he can. This will
devastate him.

Peter send me a text saying he is home and we will
talk later when I get home and not to worry.
Typical Peter!!!

Just before I leave work for home, I call mum to
talk to her, as I usually do, to make sure she is ok.
She tells me Peter has called her and told me about
the results, he sounded depressed so expect Peter
to be down in the dumps.

The drive home is excruciatingly slow due to road
works and heavy commuter traffic. I eventually
get home at six-thirty pm to find a very depressed
Peter, sat very quietly in the sitting room.

 Normally he is looking out of the front window for
me to arrive and greets me at the door with a hug

and a kiss. I take him into my arms and sense that he is hurting inside. I can tell from his red rimmed eyes that he has been crying, only he won't admit it. It's very rare to see this as he is normally such a strong and positive man.

 I hold him tightly and whisper in his ear that we should discuss in full what Mr. Khan has said and analyses it. I go and get him a G&T – his favorite drink, and we sit in front of the fire, and he retraces the whole conversation with the Consultant. Although I knew this was going to be the result, I still find it hard to comprehend, that he will never be 100% better. Deep down I had a fear and an inkling that he would be left with something, as we had been warned by the previous consultants and doctors at his past reviews, this still came as a bit of a shock ….. well not so much a shock but a disappointment as I had hoped that he would have made a full recovery.

So I need to search for all the positives to help him through this.

We end up talking for a long time that night – in between getting a bite to eat and downing a few more G&T's (V&T's in my case!).

We formulate a plan for our future life together.

Peter

Sarah is unquestionably a super human being, I am so lucky to have met her, and married her and I love her so much.

My stroke review was a hard punch in the guts, and at the same time a huge wakeup call.

Hello …. Welcome to the rest of your life!!

Let's look on the positive side.

I am on benefits due to my illness, and these will run hopefully until I retire at 66 – four years' time. Otherwise I am not sure what I can do from an employment point with my current condition.

By this time my private pension will have matured, as well as whatever government pension there is to have, so I am hoping that Sarah can either go part time or give up work totally.

I can work as a volunteer part time The Arts & Heritage Centre, and run the Flying School as well, in my own time and when I feel up to it. This will keep my brain active and an interest in my life.

I can drive my car – locally, not on long distances. I can use the train with my Senior Rail Card for anything further or have Sarah and friends drive me.

We have a lovely home, with a beautiful garden that I can sit in and admire (and cut the lawn – but nothing else!).

I can read and I can write – so I could become a published author – eventually – something to aim for maybe?

I have my health back – apart from the remanence of the stroke, and I can learn to live around my afflictions and tiredness. I will probably live to a very old age, heaven forbid!!

I have a lot of very good friends and neighbors, so our social life will always be great.

And ….. I can do all the things I love doing, apart for one thing; I can't fly on my own again!

But I can fly with my instructors or friends who hold valid pilot licenses, so it's not that bad!!

November turns out to be a busy month, with lots going on. My sister-in-law, Jane's 50th birthday celebrations, and we take Sarah's mum on a surprise visit to Coronation Street in Manchester before they close the tour for good. It was a very wet day interspersed with some dry spells that came as we finished the inside studio tour and walked the hallowed 'Street' looking at all the now very familiar houses and of course the Rovers Return. What…. you ask? Yes – sadly I am a Corro fan!!

Betty and Sarah also thoroughly enjoyed the day out and we finished with a light lunch in a local hostelry, before making our way home again.

A very significant event was the purchase of our rental aircraft for the flying school. It made total sense to buy it as the owner was retiring and gave us first option. We managed to raise the finances and now it's an asset for the flying school.

I also take the opportunity to go flying with a friend on a trip to Peterborough and he lets me fly back to Humberside – it was a bright sunny day and I thoroughly enjoyed the flight back. I checked first with our CEO and my friend agreed to be Pilot-in-Command, but let me fly from the left hand seat. We routed over the Larkenshire countryside to the coast up to Grimswell and back to our home base. Oh Great joy!!

I am kept so busy with everything that I don't have time to think about the stroke, only I do get very tired by mid-afternoons.

So my routine is to make a cup of tea and rest in our sitting room with my trusty HP laptop on my knee and I write. This is my second book and I get huge satisfaction from pouring what's in my head onto the key board and a word document.

Well you will be the judge of that!!! So if you are still reading this then I have at least held your attention so far.

Christmas is just around the corner, and I have a few weeks to think of and buy Sarah and her family some gifts and of course my own sister and family. Mostly internet shopping as I do get very weary walking around shops in the main cities and towns. The festivities also bring with them numerous invitations to dinner parties and our good friends' houses.

I am slowly coming to terms with the residue of my stroke, the consultant words still echo in my brain. He is right though; I do need to 'just get on with life'.

I make a pact with myself to be positive and satisfied with my lot.

Look at it this way: I am reasonably healthy …. Need to lose a few pounds ….. and I keep my mind active with my voluntary work at the Centre and the Airport, and I have found my new hobby of writing. My main role is as a 'house husband' to Sarah, who goes out and works long hours, on her feet all day. I want her to come home to a stress free house, where she does not have to do anything, and can just relax with a V&T, a hot bath and a deliciously cooked meal. I will do all the chores as best that I can, so that the house is kept reasonably organized and tidy.

The days do pass very quickly and sometimes there is so much going on that I don't have time to wallow in self-pity. But when you have had a stroke, such as mine; keeping your brain active is all part and parcel of fending off the dreaded depression that many suffer from.

My message to all fellow stroke sufferers; Keep active, keep as mobile as possible, do something to keep the grey matter working, and above all else – don't wallow in self-pity.

Sarah

Peter is an extraordinary man. He has so much inner strength and the ability to look on every positive side, and that is what is helping him come to terms with the aftermath of his stroke.

He took the last stroke review badly as the consultant as very blunt and matter of fact – didn't hold any punches or wrap the actual message in cotton wool. Well it's the best thing for Peter, as he can come to terms with facts.

He is a great example of what one can do to aim towards as full a recovery as one can.

I do worry about him as I leave to go to work each day …. With absolutely no justification, as when I return home each night he has yet more tales of adventures that day, and I am surprised he can squeeze in the house work, cooking and ironing.

We discuss our plans for the future and he talks positively about quite a number of projects he has in mind. He has also taken to writing, finishing his first book in 4 months, although I have yet to read it. He is still passionate about the flying school and his aircraft and gets the chance occasionally to go flying. But it's becoming very doubtful that he will be able to pass the medical examination to the required standard to re-gain his pilot's license. For me it's a godsend as I don't like the idea of Peter up in the air on his own and then suffer another TIA or worse a full stroke.

He will just have to be satisfied with flying with his numerous friends who all have pilot's licenses.

Still he has another stroke review in March next year and has six months of continued development and healing, so let's just see what this brings.

I am just grateful that the man in my life has recovered from a huge ordeal and we are going to have a very happy life together as husband and wife. Peter plans to retire fully in four years' time, and wants me to go part time or retire with him, if his pension grows enough in the current economic climate.

It's something to look forward to.

Epilogue

Why have I written this book?

Well, it's partly therapeutic and partly psychological, as it helps me understand and cope what I have been through; what I am still going through; and I am hoping that through this story I can bring some closure and acceptance to my ordeal.

I am also hoping that it may provide some hope and enlighten other people who have the miss-fortune to suffer a stroke of whatever kind and intensity.

This is my own very personal experience, which has been written over the last sixteen months, from the second week in hospital when Sarah allowed me to have my i-pad.

Most of our names have been changed as have most of the local towns and villages- so that although its autobiographical, it is still semi-fictional as it protects the identities of all our friends, families and characters in this book.

I am by nature a very positive and self-motivated person, so I hope that this story gives others the belief that they too can recover and get back to some resemblance of a near normal life.

Anyone suffering a stroke, will go through differing experiences, dependent on the severity and location of the blood clot or if they have the great misfortune to have a bleed, which is much worse and more severe.

I have taken extracts from both the Stroke

Association, as well as information from the internet to give you the reader some actual facts and figures, about strokes and the two different kinds you can have ….. if you read on!!

My only hope and wish is that anyone suffering from a stroke, can find the self-motivation and determination to fight to overcome what can be a mentally debilitating illness.

I have been through bouts of deep depression; I have lost belief and hope in myself; I have worried about how my future will look like, given that I was about to embark on a new life with my gorgeous new wife. I am adjusting to my new life, and what I am able to achieve, given my disabilities and I am determined to lead as normal a life as I am allowed to.

My fellow stroke victims, you need courage, hope and self determination to reclaim an acceptable life style. Don't let depression rule your brain. And take all the help you can get from your strong dear friends and families and allow them to support you – there is no shame in that!

Good luck, and have as good a life as you can make it.

As my consultant said to me:

'……. now just get on with it! …….'

The End

Facts & Figures Behind a Stroke

This is a very complex subject and during my stay in hospital, I quizzed the Doctors and stroke Specialists about the subject. I especially learnt more about this particular illness during the three or four times when I was asked if I would be a willing 'guinea pig' for first and fourth year student doctors who came to examine me, as part of their course.

Just to put into perspective the background behind this book, here are the facts and figure which I have cribbed from the internet, especially from The Stroke Association and the NHS data.

What is a stroke?

There are two types of stroke – ischemic (blood clot which is what I had) and Hemorrhagic (bleed in the brain)

85% of all strokes are ischemic.

A stroke is a brain attack. It happens when the blood supply to part of your brain is cut off. Blood carries essential nutrients and oxygen to your brain. Without blood your brain cells can be damaged or die. This damage can have different effects, depending on where it happens in your brain. A stroke can affect the way your body works as well as how you think, feel and communicate. Ischemic strokes are caused by a blockage, cutting off the blood supply to the brain.

The blockage can be caused by a blood clot forming in an artery leading to the brain or within one of the small vessels deep inside the brain. I suffered

from a blood clot in the medulla area on the left side of my brain, just above the spinal cord. This area of the brain controls balance, sight and speech. Hemorrhagic strokes are caused when a blood vessel bursts within or on the surface of the brain. Because the blood leaks out into the brain tissue at high pressure, the damage caused can be greater than the damage caused by strokes due to a clot. There are two types of hemorrhagic stroke:
1. Intracerebral hemorrhage (ICH) – bleeding within the brain
2. Subarachnoid hemorrhage (SAH) – bleeding on the surface of the brain.
Hemorrhagic strokes are generally more severe and are associated with a considerably higher risk of mortality within three months and beyond, when compared to ischemic strokes.
A transient ischemic attack or TIA is also known as a mini-stroke. It is the same as a stroke, except that the symptoms last for a short amount of time and no longer than 24 hours. This is because the blockage that stops the blood getting to your brain is temporary.
Again I suffered a number of these mini transient ischemic attacks in the two months before my stroke, but because of my high blood sugar levels and cholesterol, these were diagnosed as the onset of diabetes, which has similar signs.

What causes stroke?
As we age our arteries become harder and narrower and more likely to become blocked.

However, certain medical conditions and lifestyle factors can speed up this process and increase your risk of having a stroke, such as a high level of stress, long working hours, the wrong food and alcohol.

Can you recover from stroke?

All strokes are different. For some people the effects may be relatively minor and may not last long. Others may be left with more serious problems that make them dependent on other people

Unfortunately, not everyone survives – around one in eight people die within 30 days of having a stroke. That's why it's so important to be able to recognize the symptoms and get medical help as quickly as possible.

The quicker you receive treatment, the better your chances for a good recovery. Make sure you know how to recognize the symptoms of stroke.

Diagnosis

A stroke is a medical emergency and if you have one you need to call 999 immediately.

You may start off in accident and emergency or another assessment ward, but it is likely you will be quickly admitted to an acute (or hyper-acute) stroke unit. An acute stroke unit has a range of trained professionals who are experienced in stroke care.

The quicker your stroke is diagnosed and treated, the better your recovery will be.

A stroke is usually diagnosed using a brain scan: either a computed tomography (CT) scan or a magnetic resonance imaging (MRI) scan. The scan will show whether your stroke has been caused by a blockage or by something else.

Treatment

If your ischemic stroke is caused by a blood clot, you may be treated with a clot-busting medicine, known as thrombolysis.

Thrombolysis can break down and disperse a clot that is preventing blood from reaching your brain. However, for it to have the best effect, it needs to be given within four and a half hours of your stroke symptoms starting.

Most people who have an ischemic stroke will be given anti-platelet medication, which helps to prevent your blood from clotting.

What Is Wallenberg Syndrome?

Wallenberg syndrome is a rare condition in which an infarction, or stroke, occurs in the lateral medulla. The lateral medulla is a part of the brain stem. When the arteries that lead to this part of the brain are blocked, oxygenated blood doesn't get to this part of the brain, and a stroke can occur. This condition is also sometimes called lateral medullary infarction. However, the cause of the syndrome isn't always clear. THIS IS WHAT I HAVE.

Symptoms of Wallenberg Syndrome

Because the brain stem is in charge of delivering messages to the spinal cord for motor and sensory function, a stroke in this area causes problems with how the person's muscles function and sensations are perceived. The most common symptom people with Wallenberg syndrome have is dysphagia, or difficulty swallowing. This can become very serious if it affects how much nutrition you are getting. Other symptoms include:

- hoarseness
- nausea and vomiting
- hiccups
- rapid eye movements (nystagmus)
- a decrease in sweating
- problems with body temperature sensation
- dizziness
- trouble walking
- trouble with maintaining your balance

In some cases, people with Wallenberg syndrome experience paralysis or numbness on one side of the body. This can occur in the limbs, in the face, or even in a small area like the tongue. You can also experience a difference in how hot or cold something is on one side of the body. Some individuals will walk at a slant or report that everything around them seems tilted or off balance. The syndrome can also cause changes in your heart rate (bradycardia) and blood pressure (hypo- and hypertension). Make sure to discuss any symptoms you have with your healthcare provider. Every bit of information can help in making the diagnosis.

How Is Wallenberg Syndrome Diagnosed?

Usually a doctor will make a diagnosis after carefully reviewing your health history and listening to the description of your symptoms. If your healthcare provider suspects that you have Wallenberg syndrome, you may undergo a computed tomography (CT) scan or magnetic resonance imaging (MRI) to confirm whether or not there is a block in the artery near the lateral medulla.

How Is Wallenberg Syndrome Treated?

There is no cure for this condition, but your healthcare provider will probably focus treatment on relieving or eliminating your symptoms. He or she may prescribe speech and swallowing therapy to help you learn to swallow again. If your situation is severe, your doctor may recommend a feeding tube so you can get the nutrients you need. In some cases, you may be prescribed medication. You may be given pain medication if you have chronic or long-lasting pain. A blood thinner, such as heparin or warfarin, may be prescribed to help reduce or dissolve the blockage in the artery. This can also help to prevent future blood clots from forming. Sometimes an anti-epileptic or anti-seizure drug called gabapentin can help with the symptoms. In extreme cases, surgery may be an option to remove the clot. This is not a common form of a treatment, however, because of the difficulty of getting to that area of the brain. Make sure to discuss your treatment options with your healthcare provider and follow the plan carefully.

What Is the Long-Term Outlook for Wallenberg Syndrome?

Although the diagnosis and symptoms can be frightening, the long-term outlook for Wallenberg syndrome is actually fairly positive. How well you recover depends on where the stroke happened in the brainstem, as well as how much damage occurred. Some people can recover between a few weeks to six months after treatment. Others with more significant damage may have trouble or more permanent disabilities. You should discuss your long-term outlook with your healthcare provider if you have any questions. Be sure to follow your treatment plan carefully so you can make a successful recovery.

Statistics:

• Stroke kills twice as many women as breast cancer and more men than prostate and testicular cancer combined a year.

• Black people are twice as likely to have a stroke compared to white people.

• Black and South Asian people have strokes at a younger age compared to white people.

• Stroke is one of the largest causes of disability – half of all stroke survivors have a disability.

• Over a third of stroke survivors in the UK are dependent on others, of those 1 in 5 are cared for by family and/or friends.

• Stroke occurs approximately 152,000 times a year in the UK; that is one every 3 minutes 27 seconds.

• First-time incidence of stroke occurs almost 17 million times a year worldwide; one every two seconds.

• There are over 1.2 million stroke survivors in the UK.

• 3 in 10 stroke survivors will go on to have a recurrent stroke or TIA.

• 1 in 8 strokes are fatal within the first 30 days.

• 1 in 4 strokes are fatal within a year.

• 1 in 12 people will have a stroke within a week of having a TIA
• Approximately 10,000 recurrent strokes can be prevented every year in the UK if TIA and minor strokes are treated in time.
• Stroke is the fourth single largest cause of death in the UK and second in the world.
• By the age of 75, 1 in 5 women and 1 in 6 men will have a stroke.

About Depression ..... What Is Depression?

Depression is a mood disorder characterized by low mood and a wide range of other possible symptoms, which will vary from person to person. This illness can develop quickly or gradually, and be brought on by life events and/or changes in body chemistry. It can strike anyone, and is curable in very many cases.

Some experts look upon depression as a defense mechanism that one's body adopts in order to escape from unbearable stress. In some cases, it could even be a form of anger directed towards the self for not having lived up to one's expectations, which may well have been set too high in the first place.

What Are The Signs Of Depression?

The signs of depression are many, because this soul-destroying illness affects each person differently, and in its degree of severity. You may be suffering from depression if, for a long time, you experience several of the following symptoms:

•Sadness and feeling weepy.

- Numbness, lethargy and a loss of interest in things and activities you used to enjoy.
- Wanting to hide away from people, perhaps even by staying in bed.
- Constant tiredness and problems sleeping.
- Loss of appetite, or eating to excess for the comfort it may bring.
- Stress and frustration.
- Irritability and aggression.
- Feeling that you cannot cope.
- Inability to see any glimmer of a 'light at the end of the tunnel'.
- Asking yourself what the point of living is

Glossary

• **Aphasia:** Aphasia (sometimes called dysphasia) is a language disorder caused by stroke. It can affect speech, comprehension and reading and writing skills.

• **Hyper-acute stroke unit:** Specialist centers to manage the first 72 hours of stroke care.

• **Onset:** When the symptoms of stroke fist started. Also referred to medically as 'ictus'.

• **Thrombolysis:** A clot-busting treatment to dissolve the clot and restore blood flow. Also referred to as 'rt-PA' and 'alteplase'.

• **Door to needle:** The time it takes from admission to hospital (door) to administering thrombolysis treatment (needle).

• **Early supported discharge (ESD):** Designed for stroke survivors with mild to moderate disability who can be discharged home from hospital sooner to receive the necessary therapy at home.

• **Ischemic stroke:** A stroke caused by a clot.

• **Hemorrhagic stroke:** A stroke caused by a bleed.

• **Transient ischemic attack (TIA):** Sometimes referred to as a 'mini-stroke' or 'warning stroke' – an event is defined as a TIA if the symptoms resolve within 24 hours.

• **ABCD2 score:** ABCD2 is predictive tool used to assess the short-term risk of stroke after a TIA.

• **Incidence:** The number of stroke occurrences.

• **Prevalence:** The number of living stroke survivors.

• **Mortality:** The number of deaths caused by stroke.

• **Epidemiology:** The study and research of how often a disease occurs in people and why.

The Stroke
'..... just get on with it .....'

'This story is based on fact, from a personal experience, however the names of all the people depicted in this story have been changed as have the location and place names'

So any resemblance to names, people, characters, locations, organisations, businesses, places, events or incidents are totally and purely co-incidental and a product of the authors imagination.

Written by Chris Dale
chris@mydale.co.uk

May 2016

2nd Edition   June 2016

ABOUT THE AUTHOR

Chris Dale was born in Lima, Peru in January 1954, came to the UK in 1964 for a public school education, and staid in the UK after his education. Chris is now 62, and spent all of his working life in commercial sales & marketing roles, starting in the airline business, then moving into sales, marketing and buying roles in branded food manufacturing and retail food industry, latterly running his own consultancy business. He was a pilot and still owns and runs a successful flying school. In July 2014 he suffered a serious stroke, which forced semi-retirement, and thus he found the joy of writing, with this is his first book. He started this whilst still in hospital on his iPad on Verdana font 28 as he had severe double vision at the time. His first 14,000 word booklet has been published by the NHS Trust to help other stroke suffers come to terms with their condition. This is based on that initial booklet but expanded into a semi-biographical/fiction book, with the names and locations changed.

Made in the USA
Charleston, SC
25 October 2016